This Book Belongs to

COLOR TEST PAGE

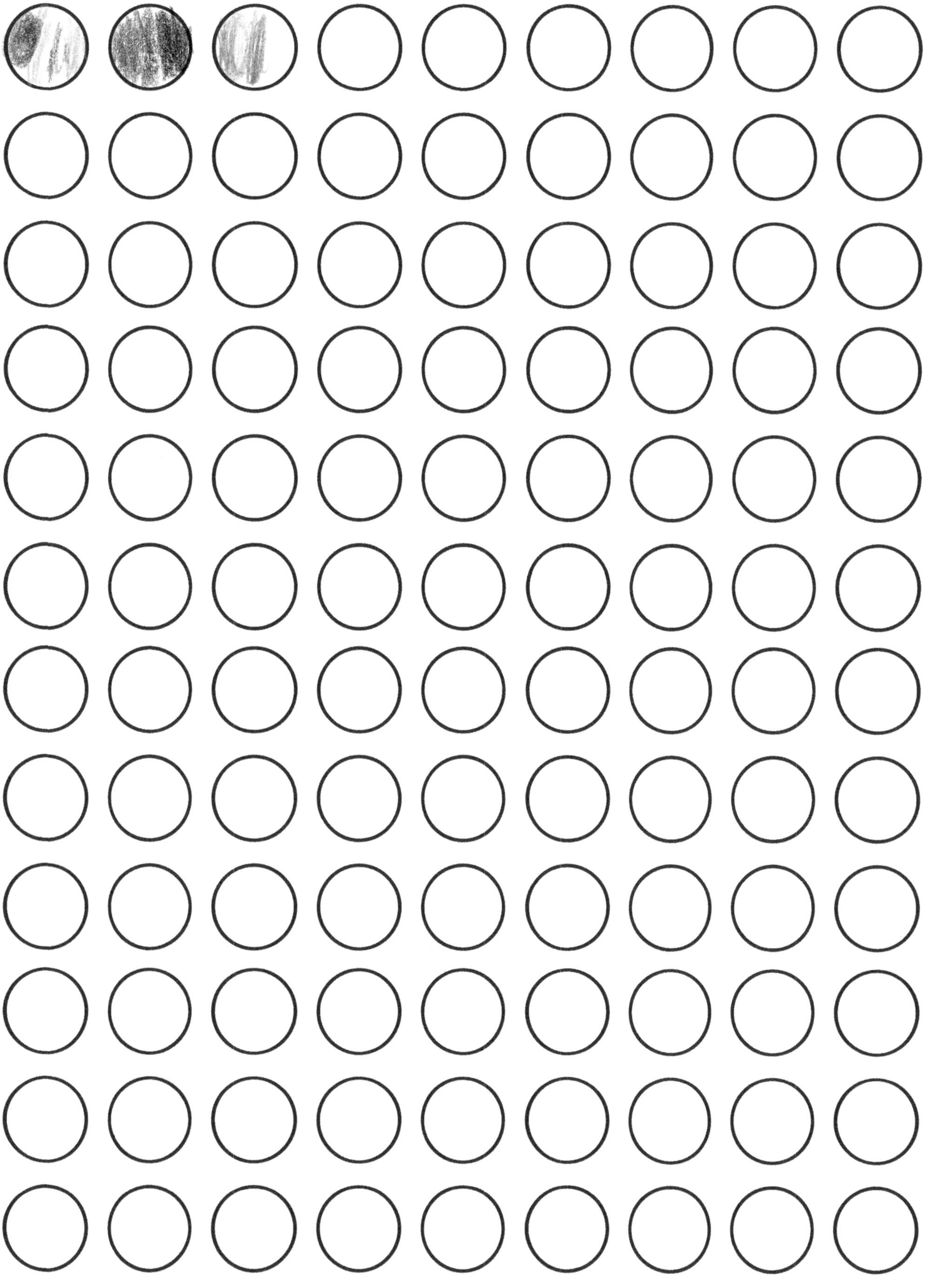

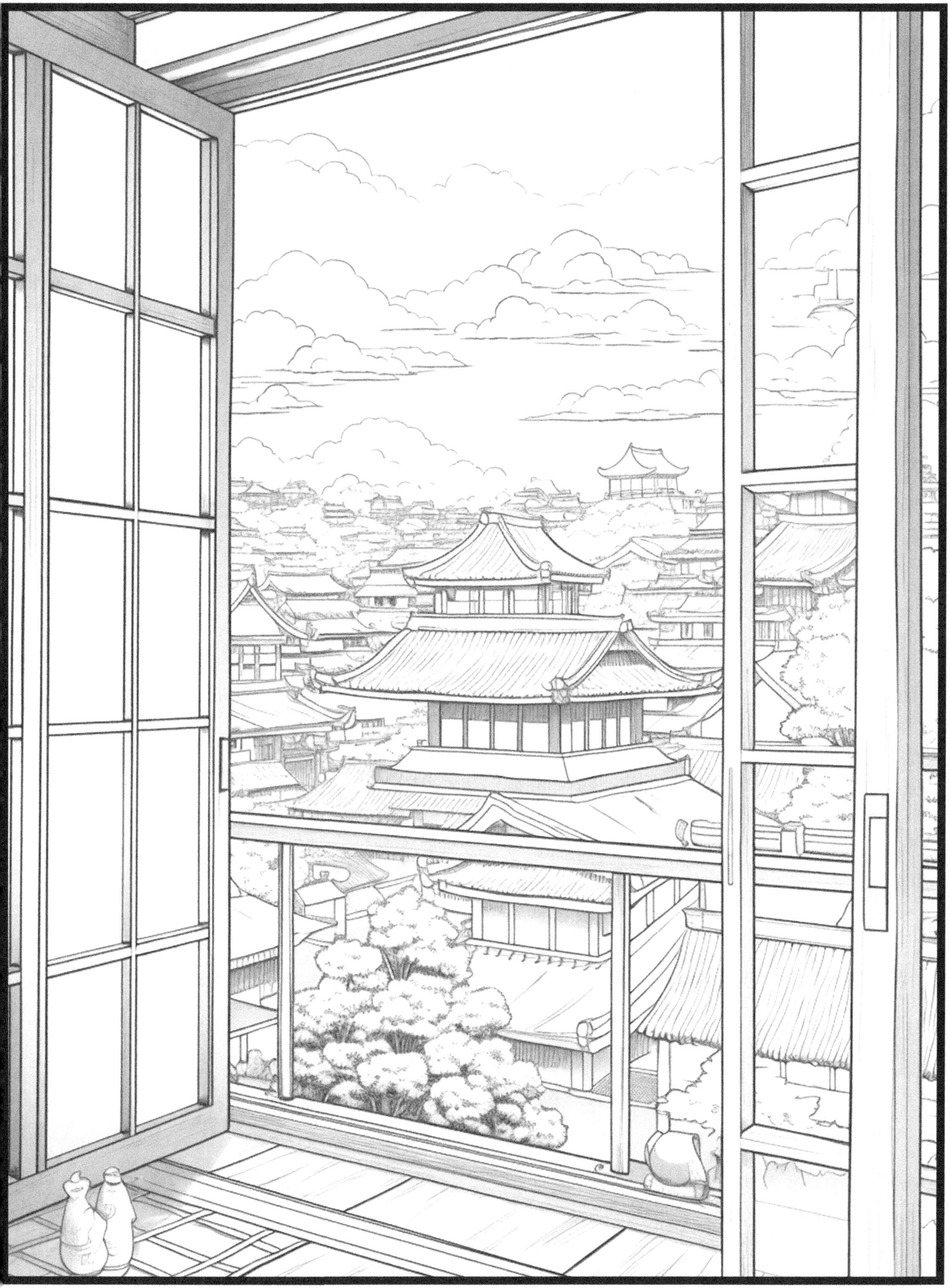

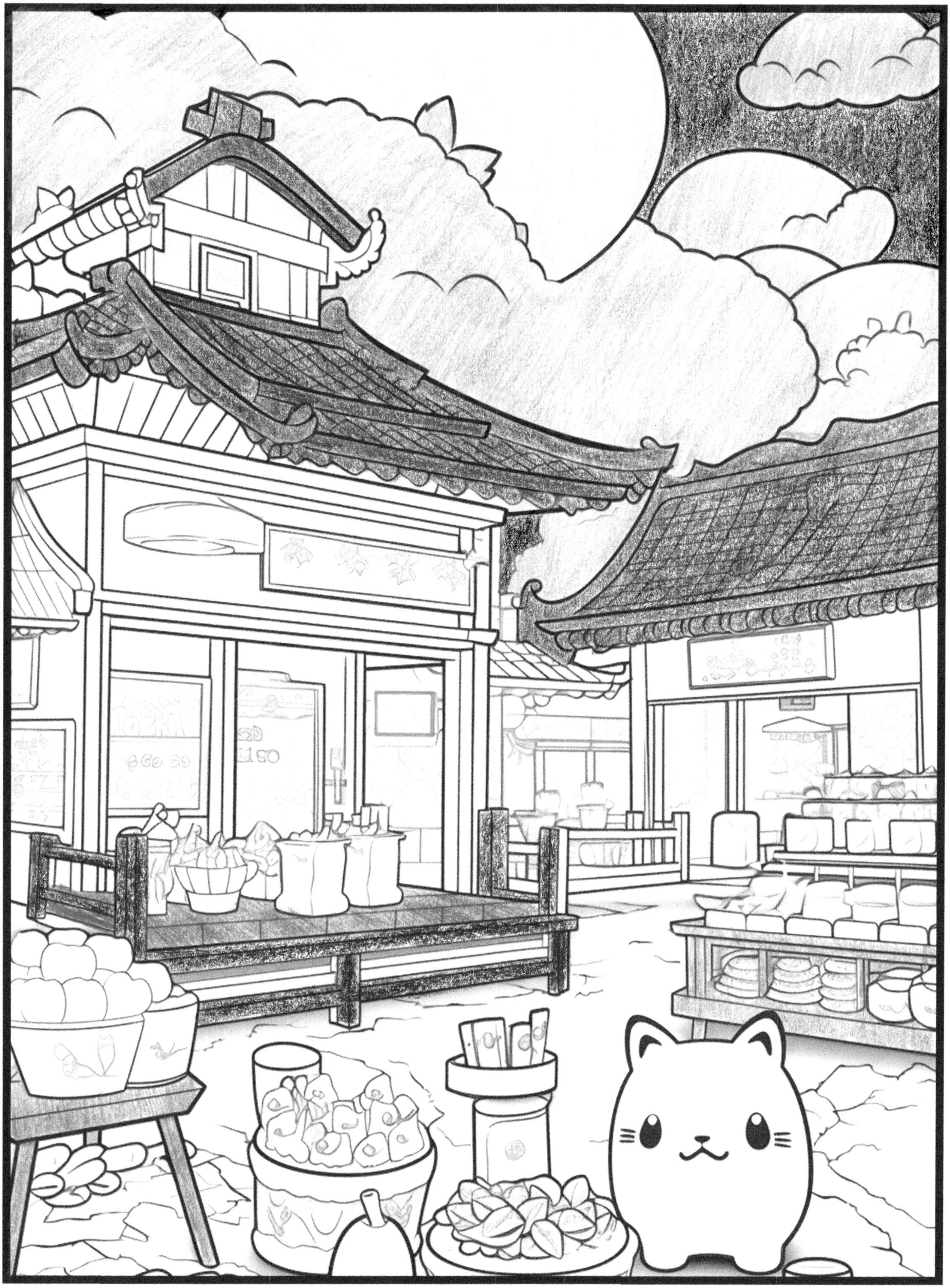

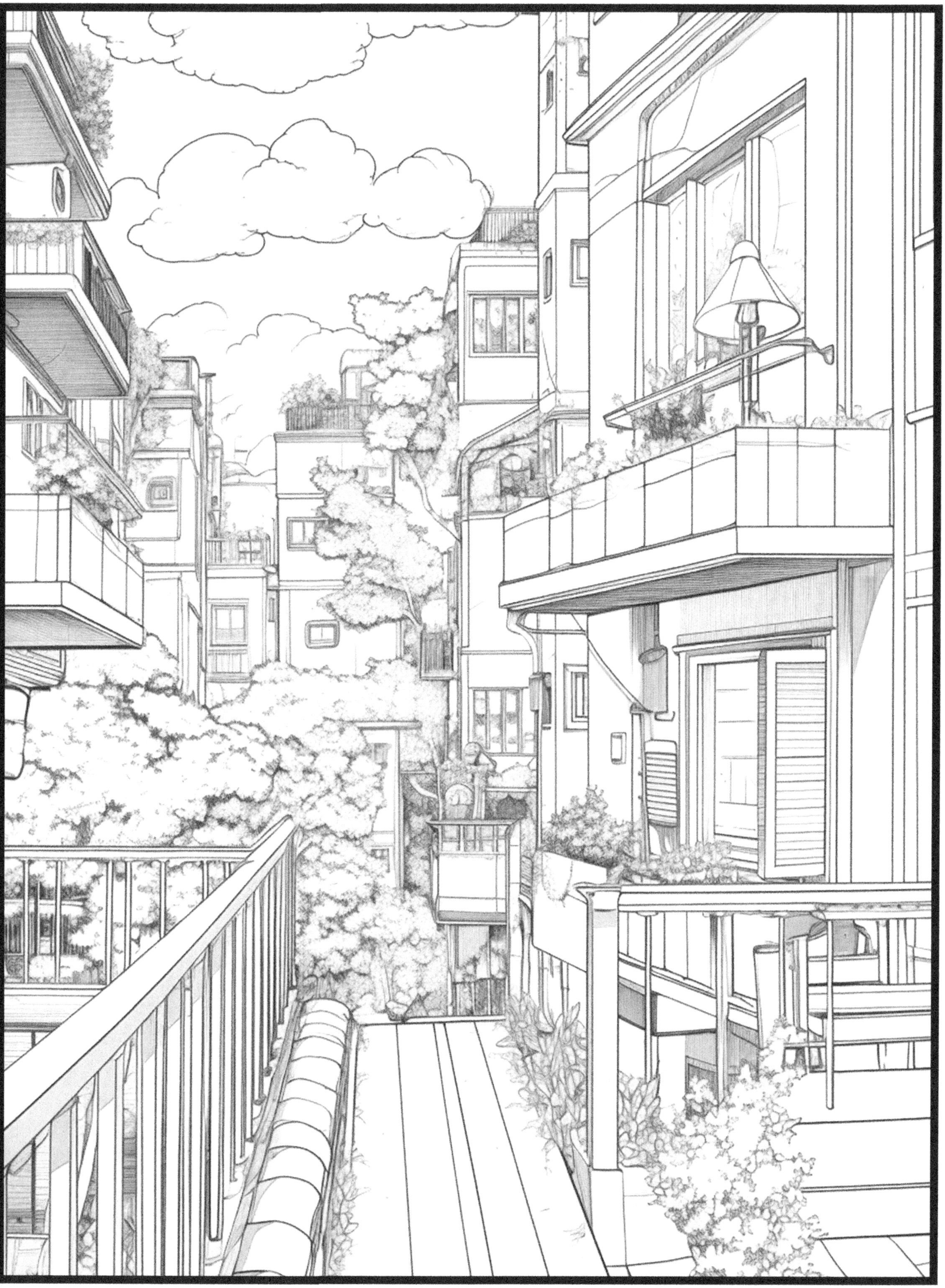

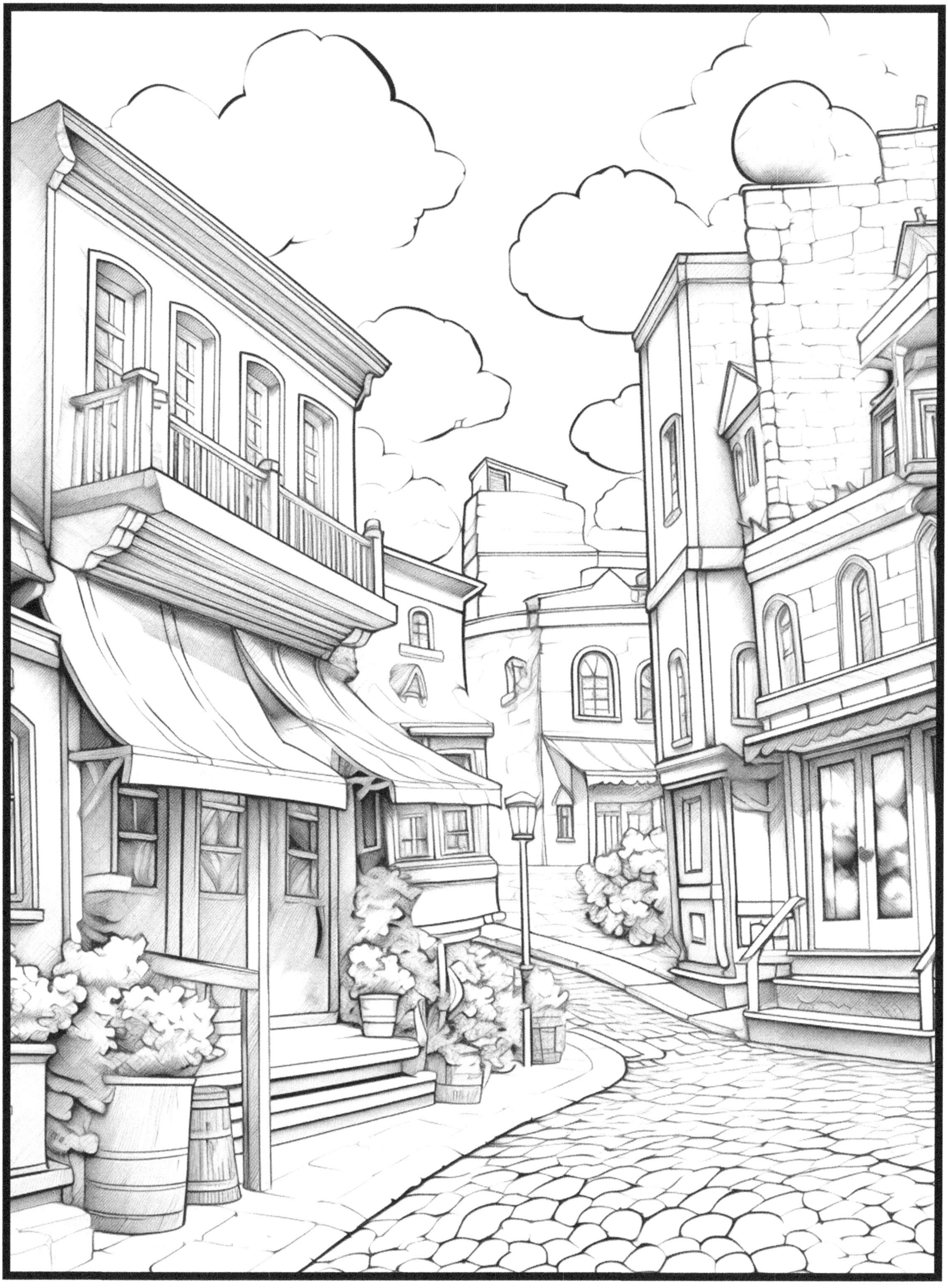
A

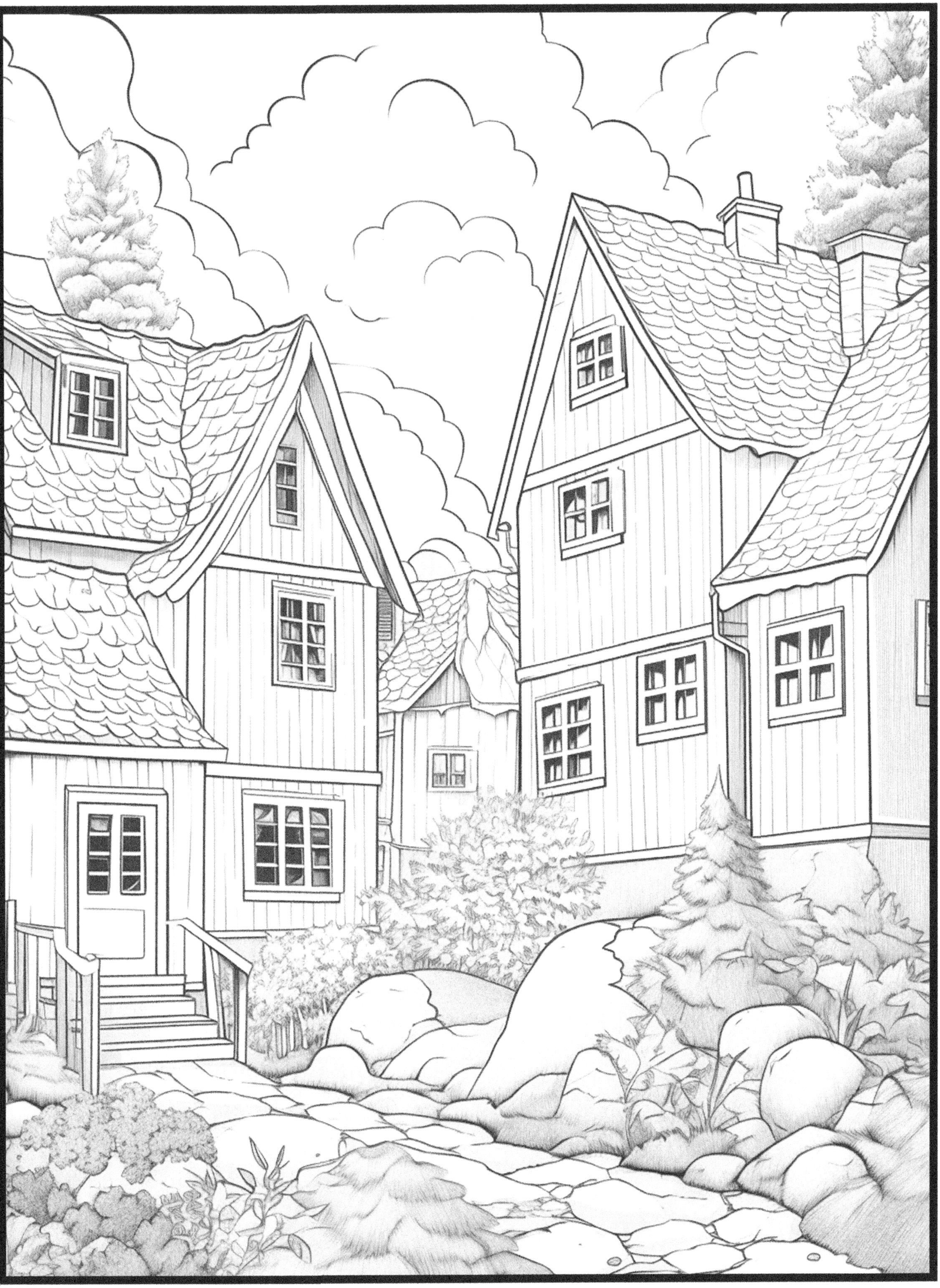

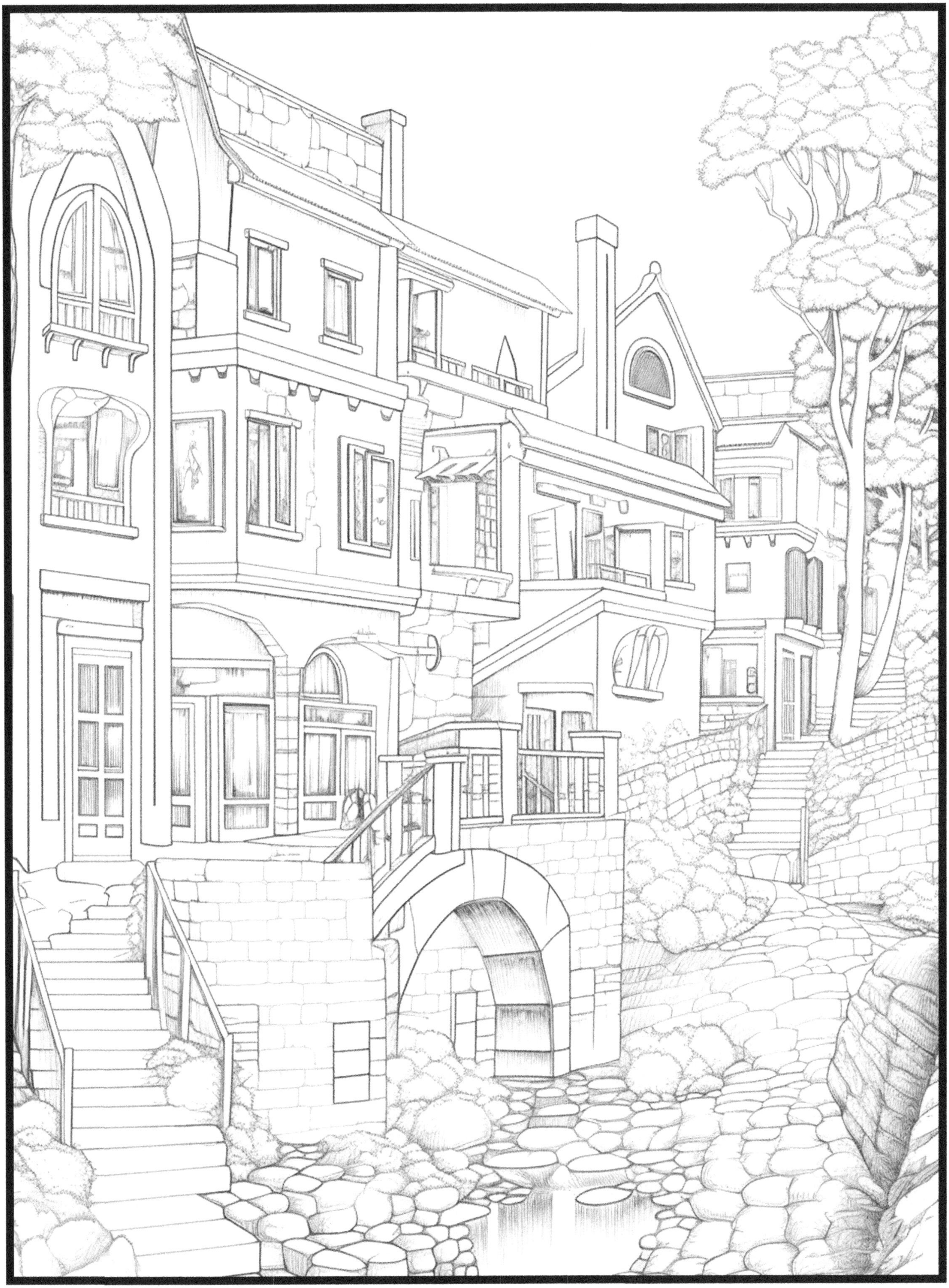

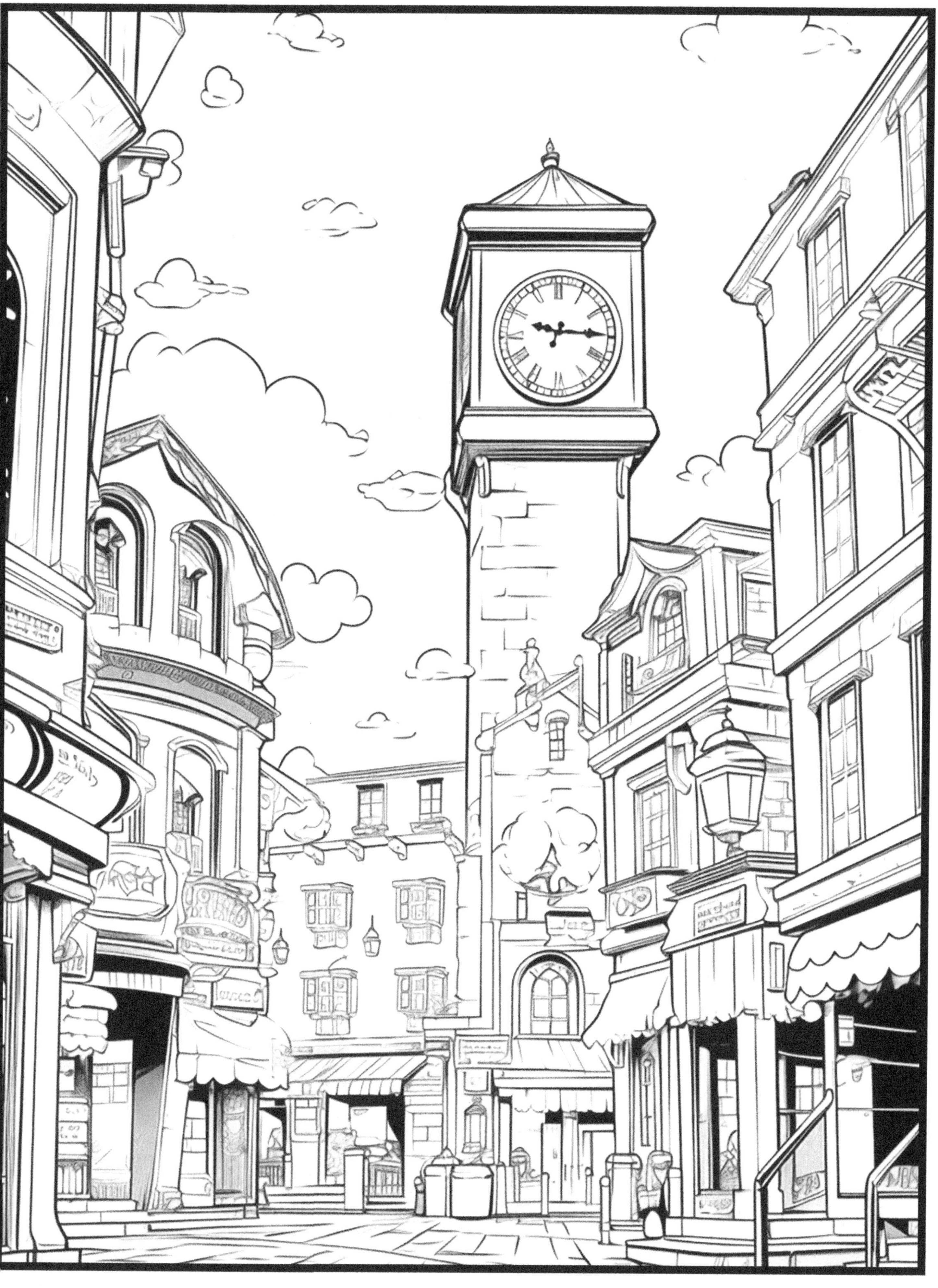

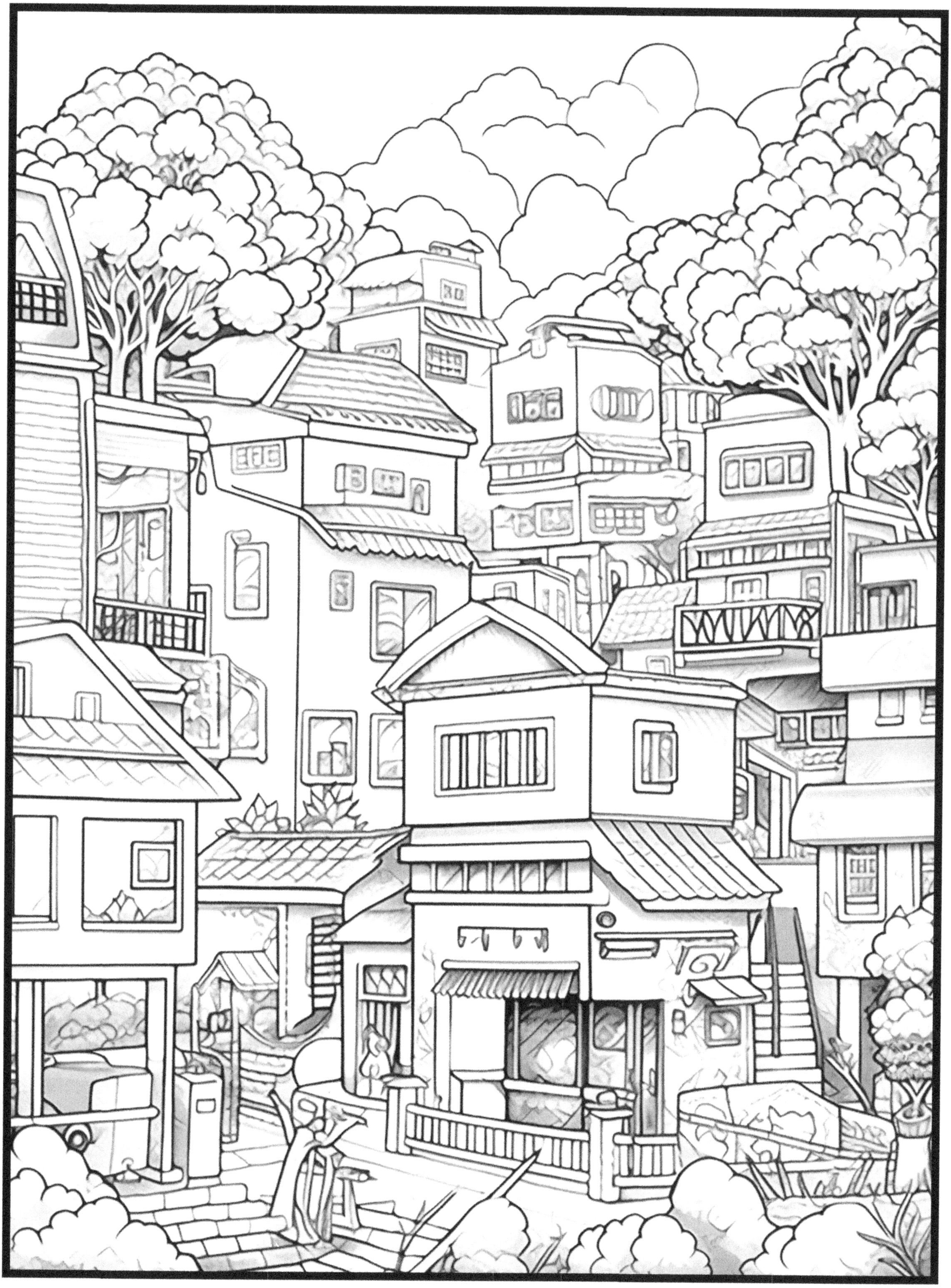

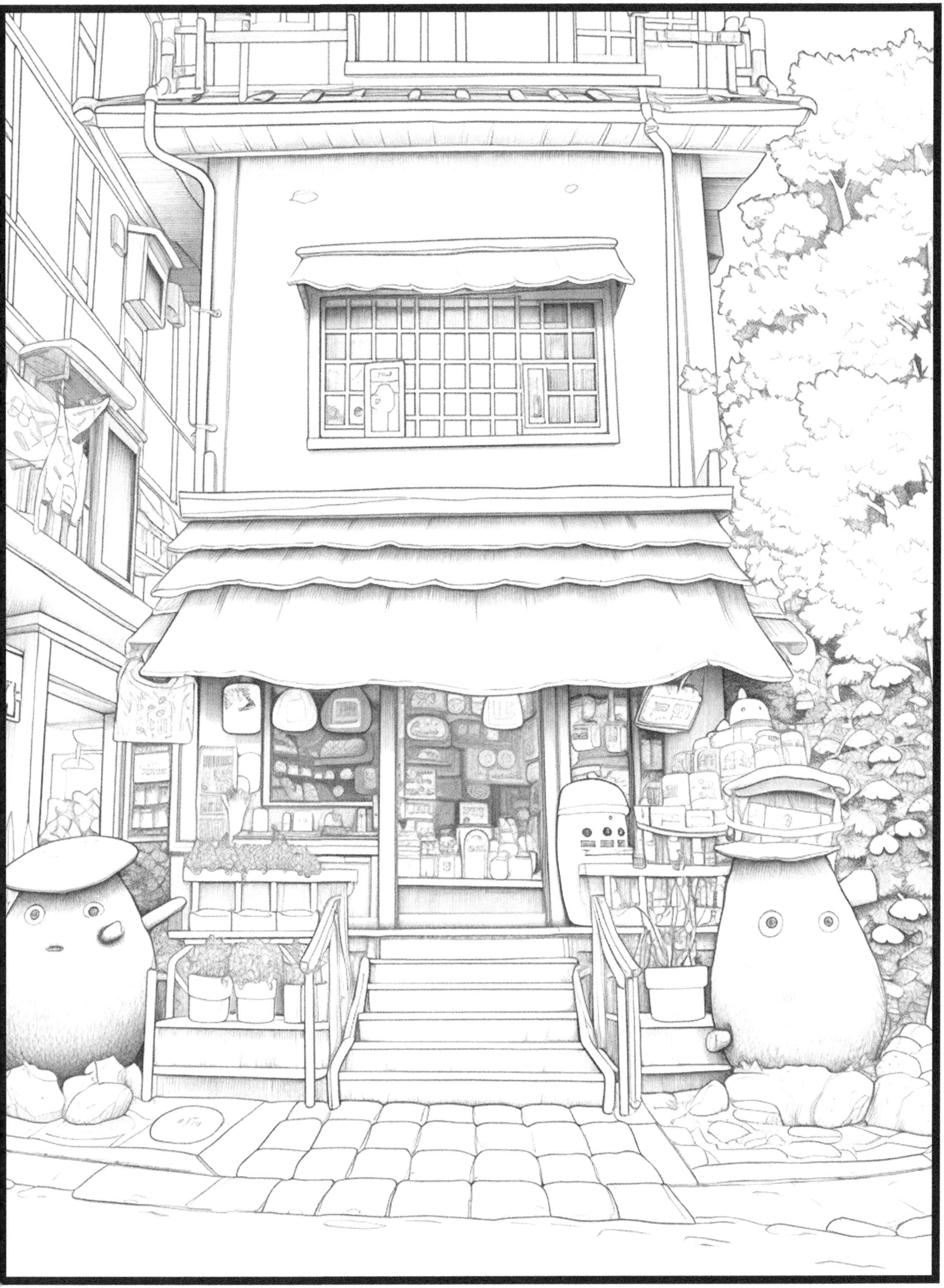

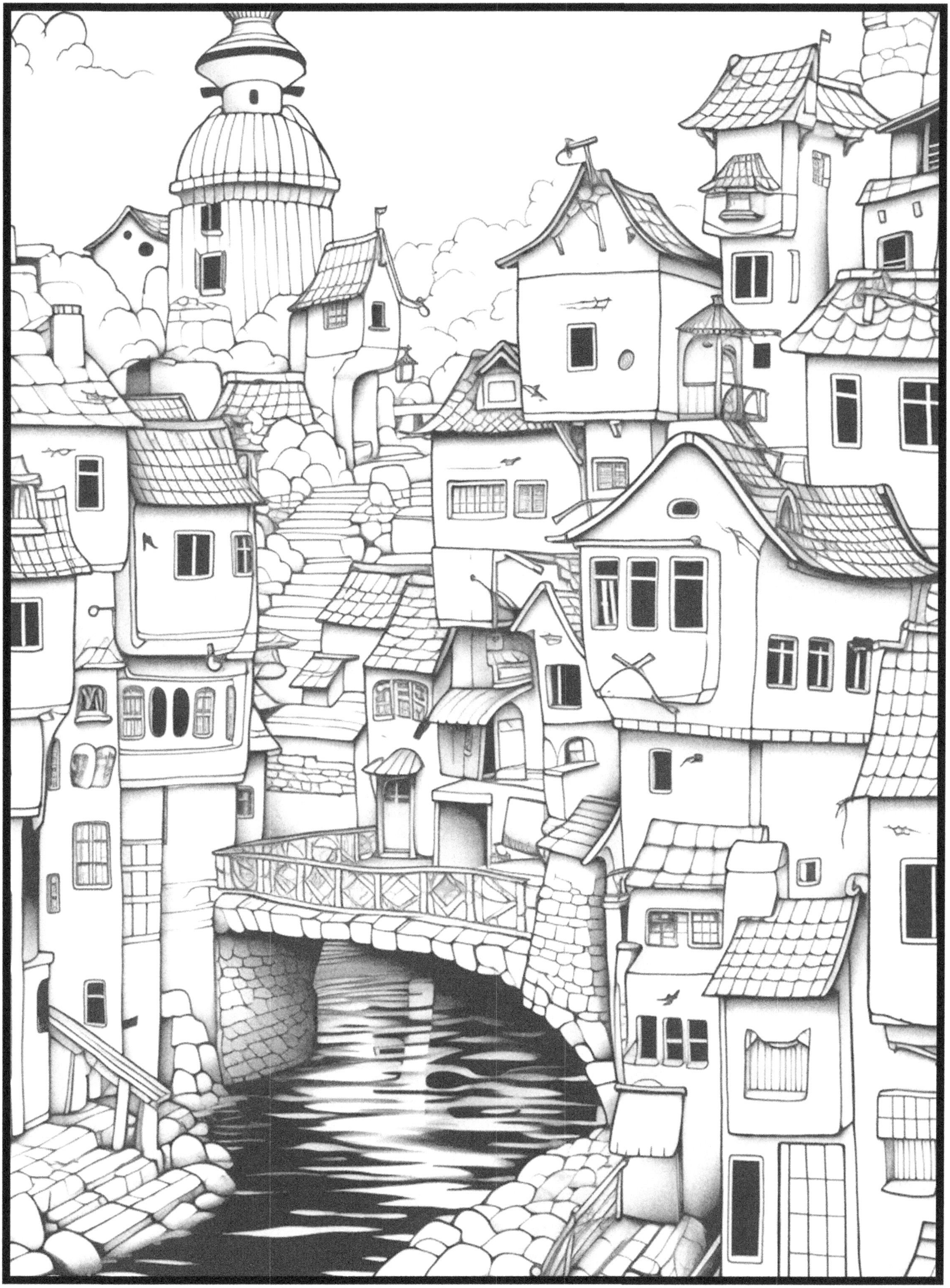

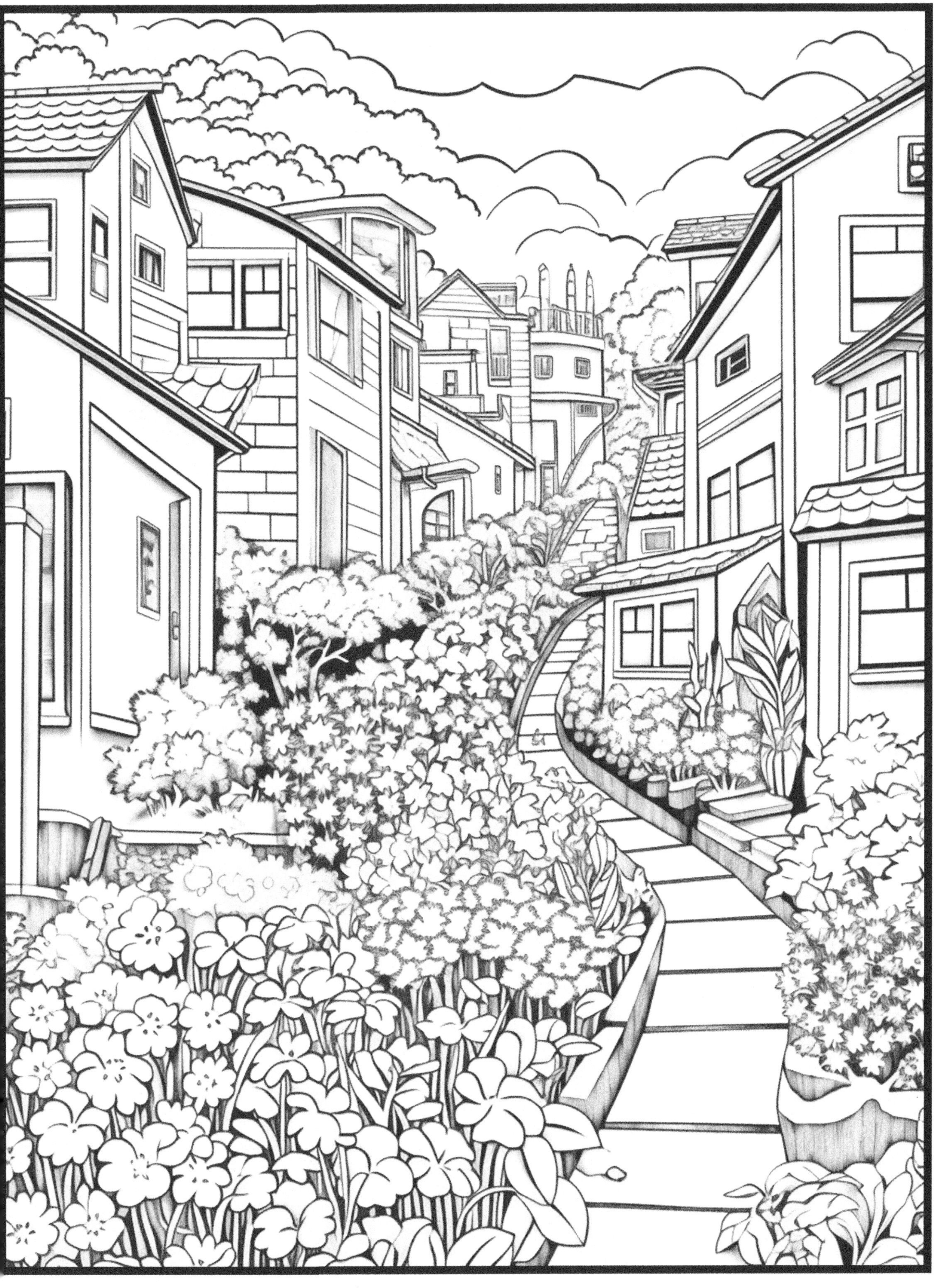

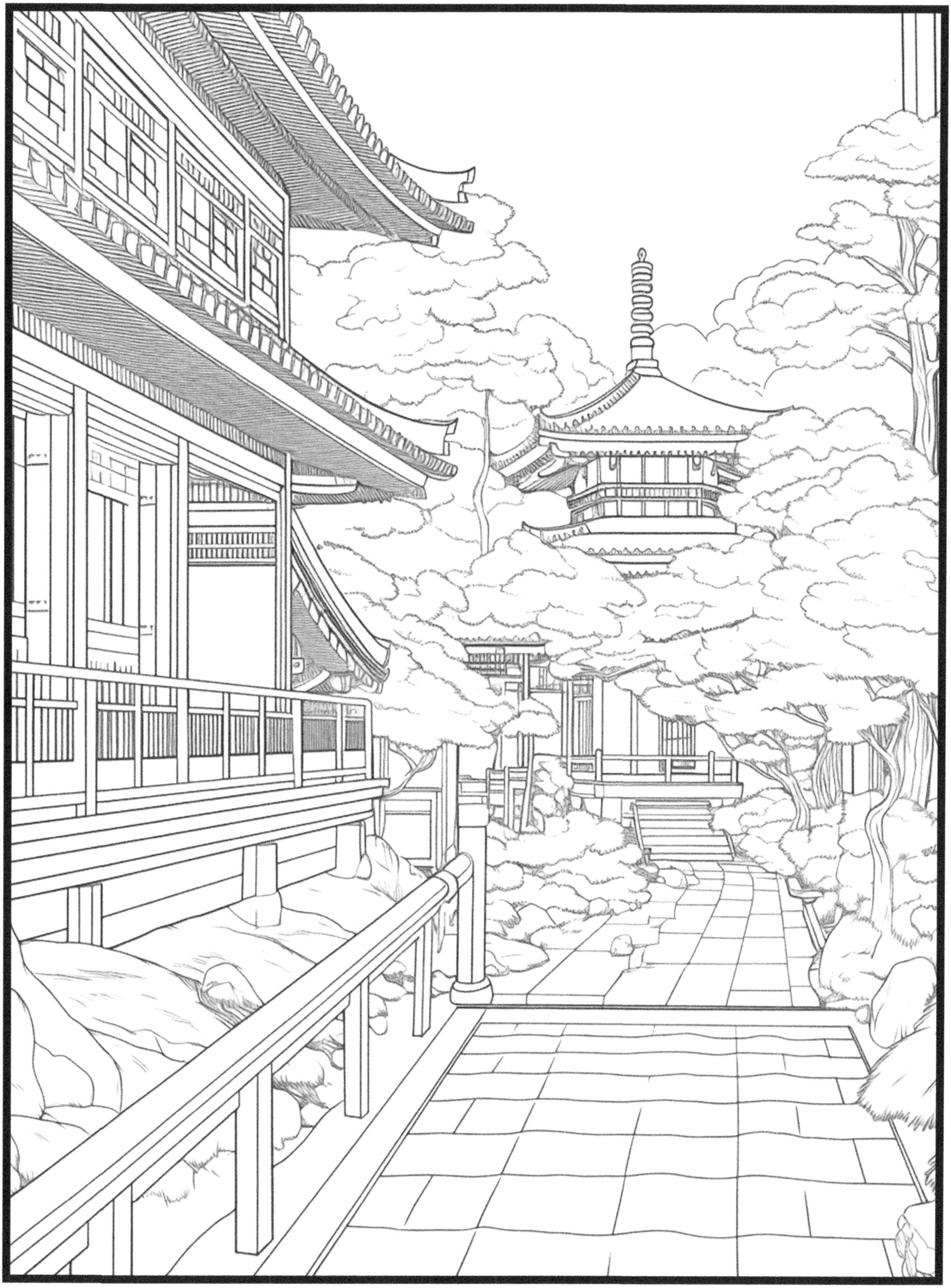

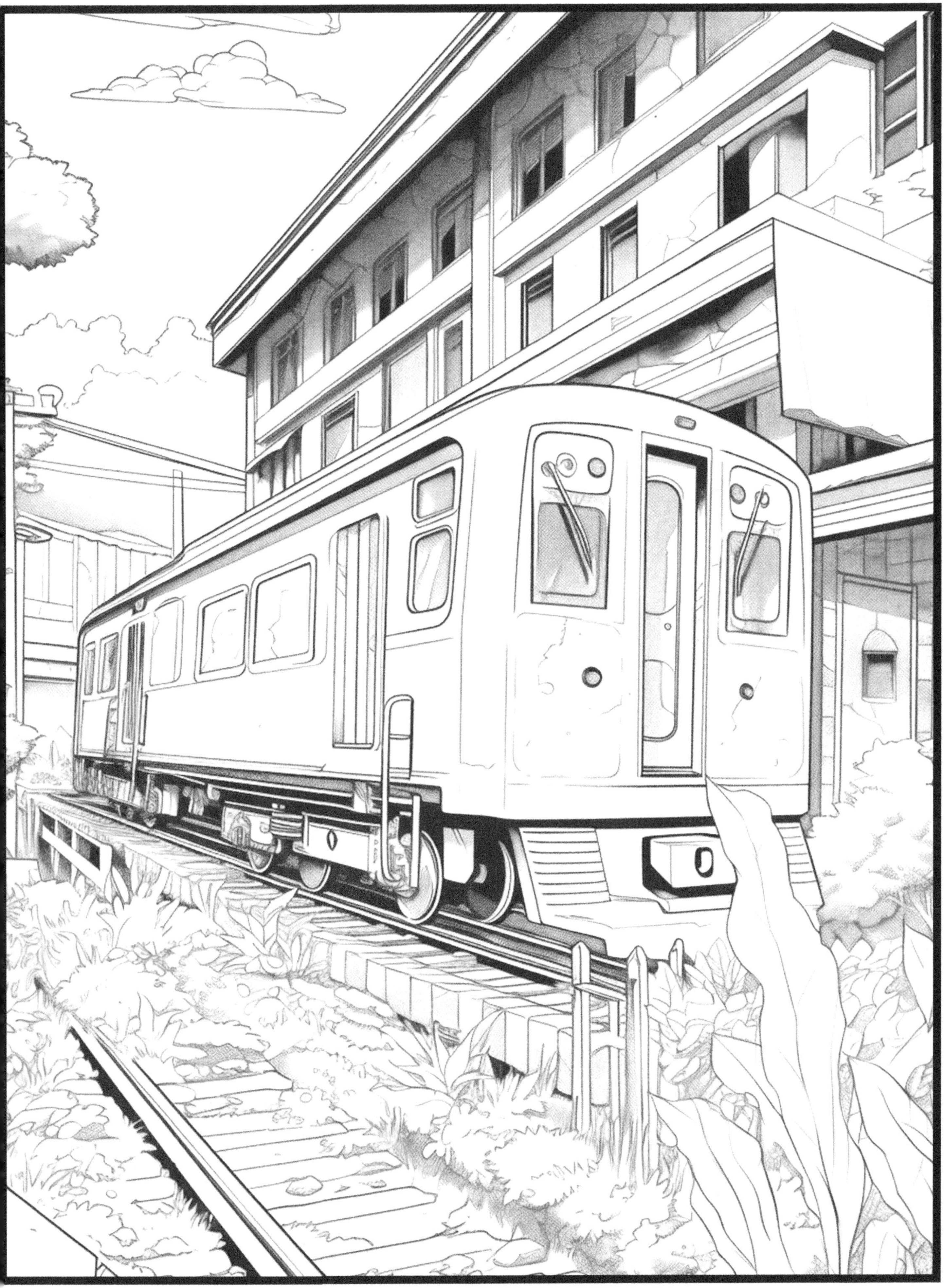

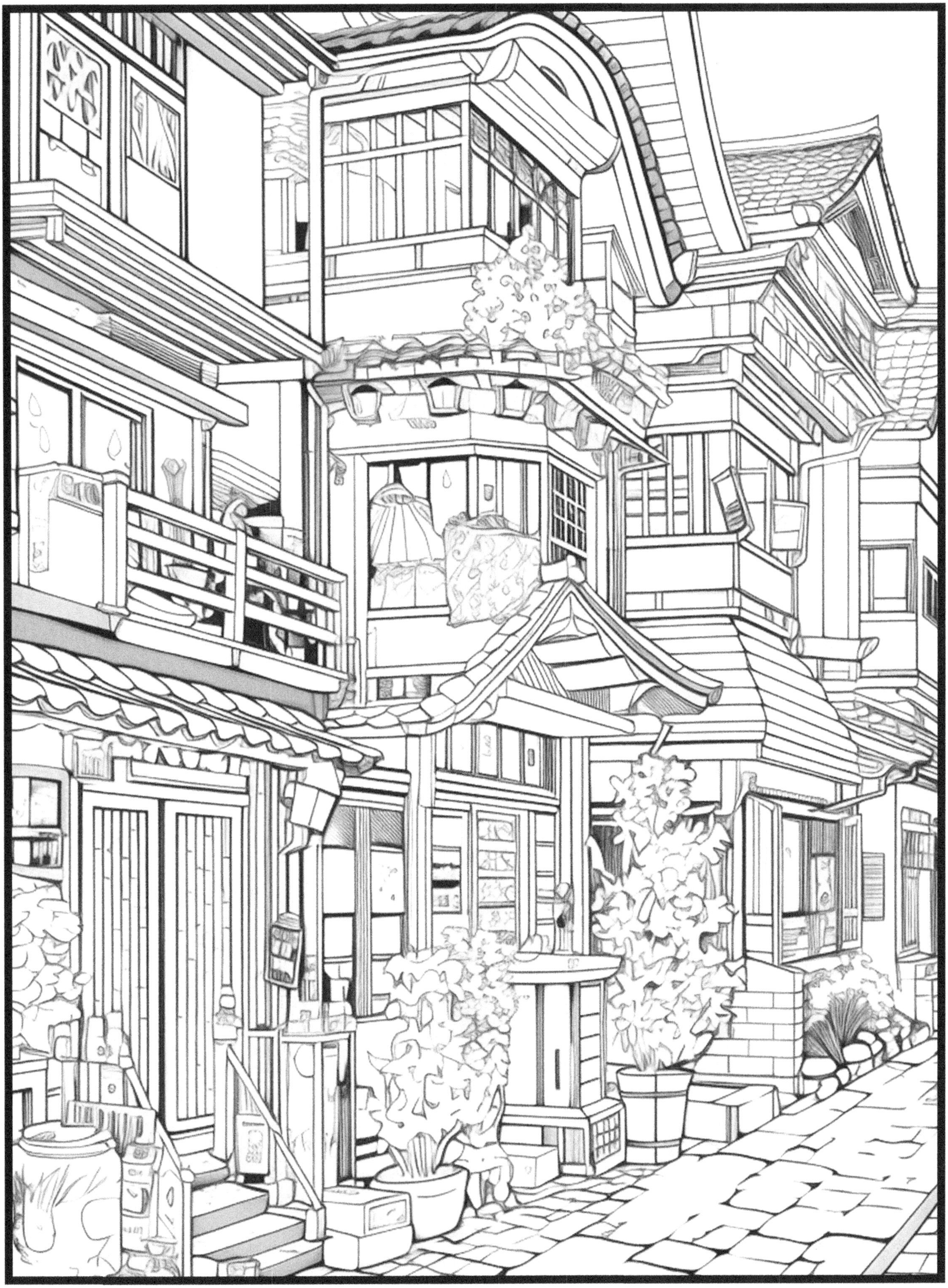

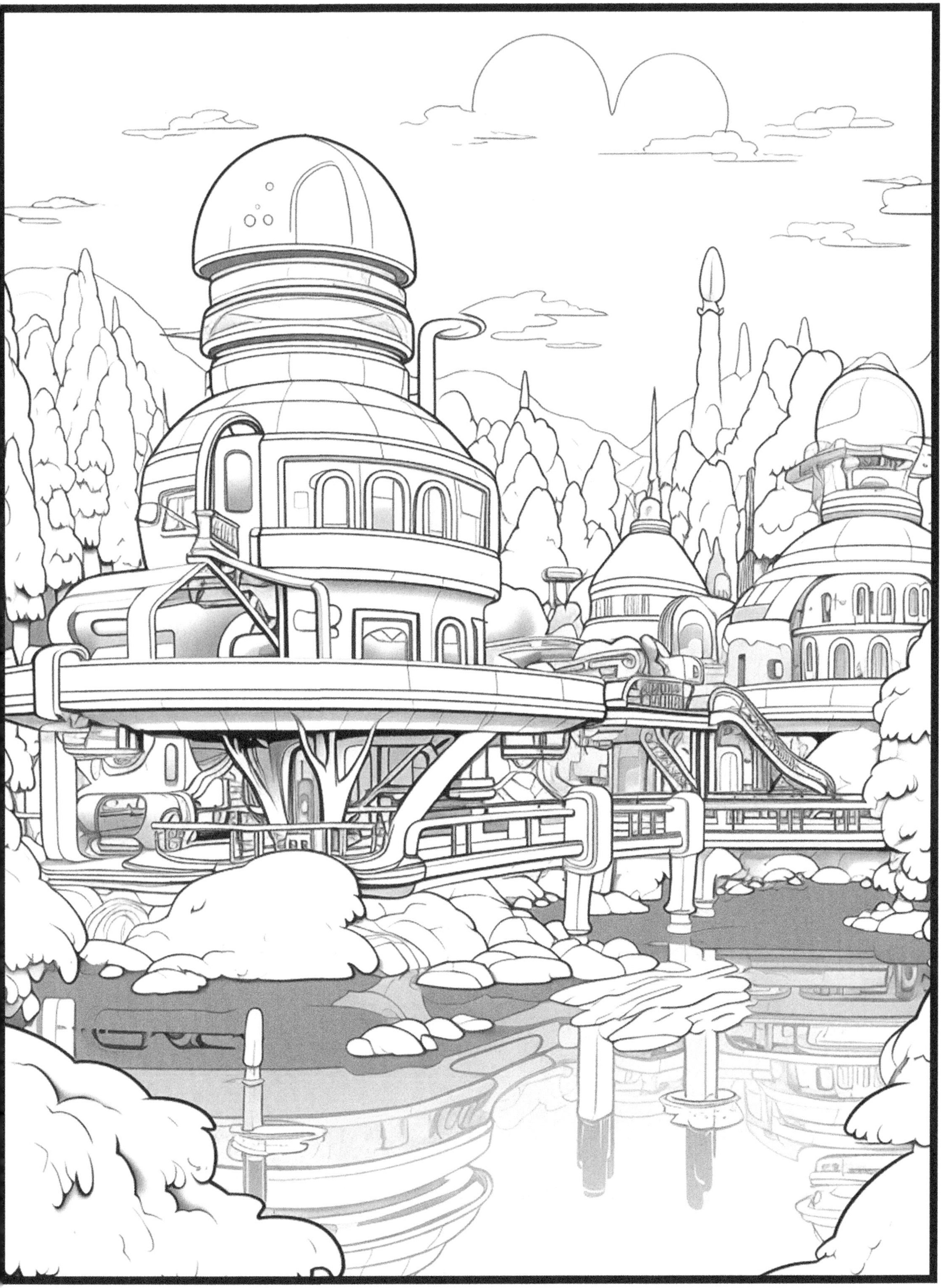

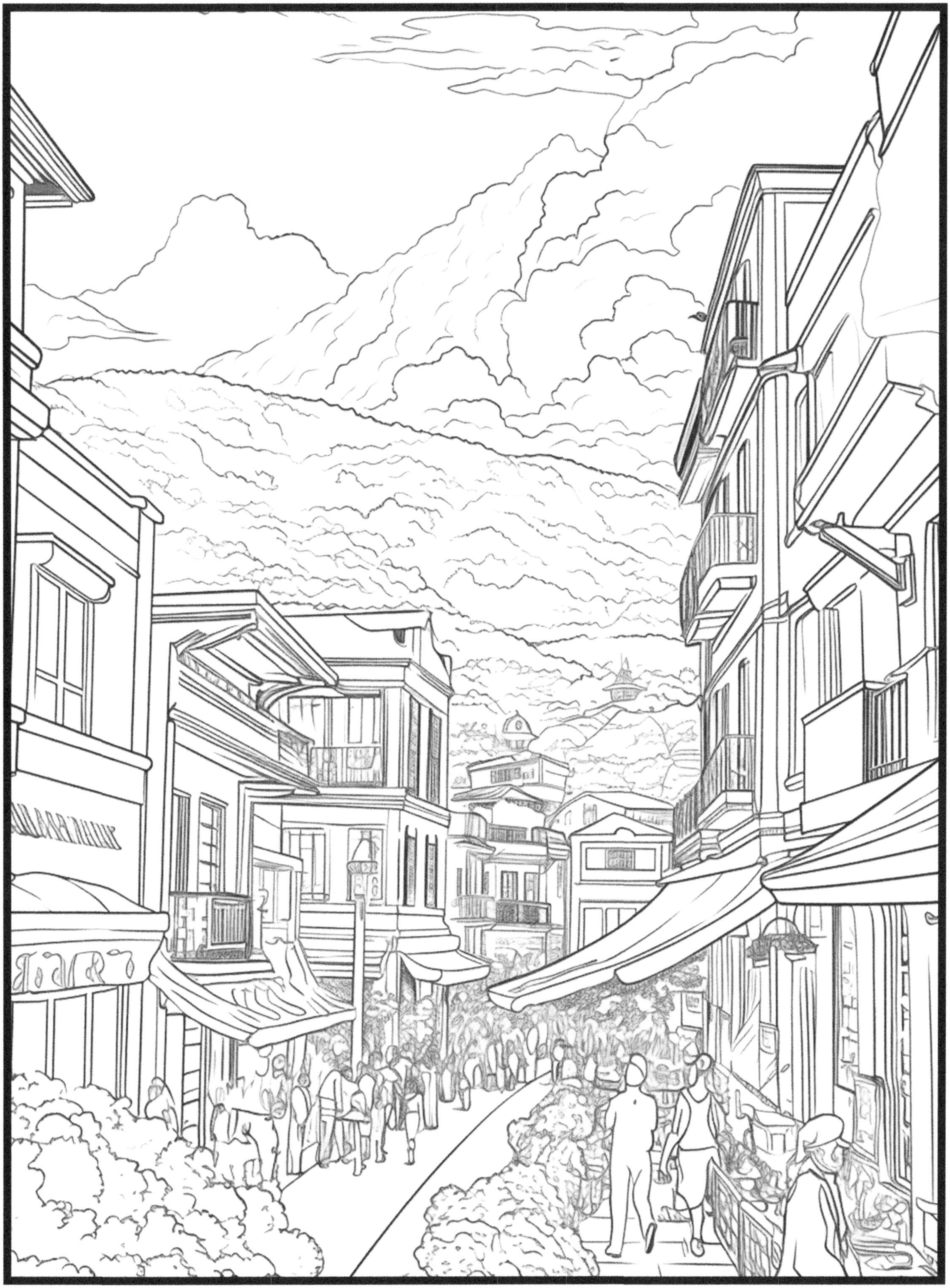

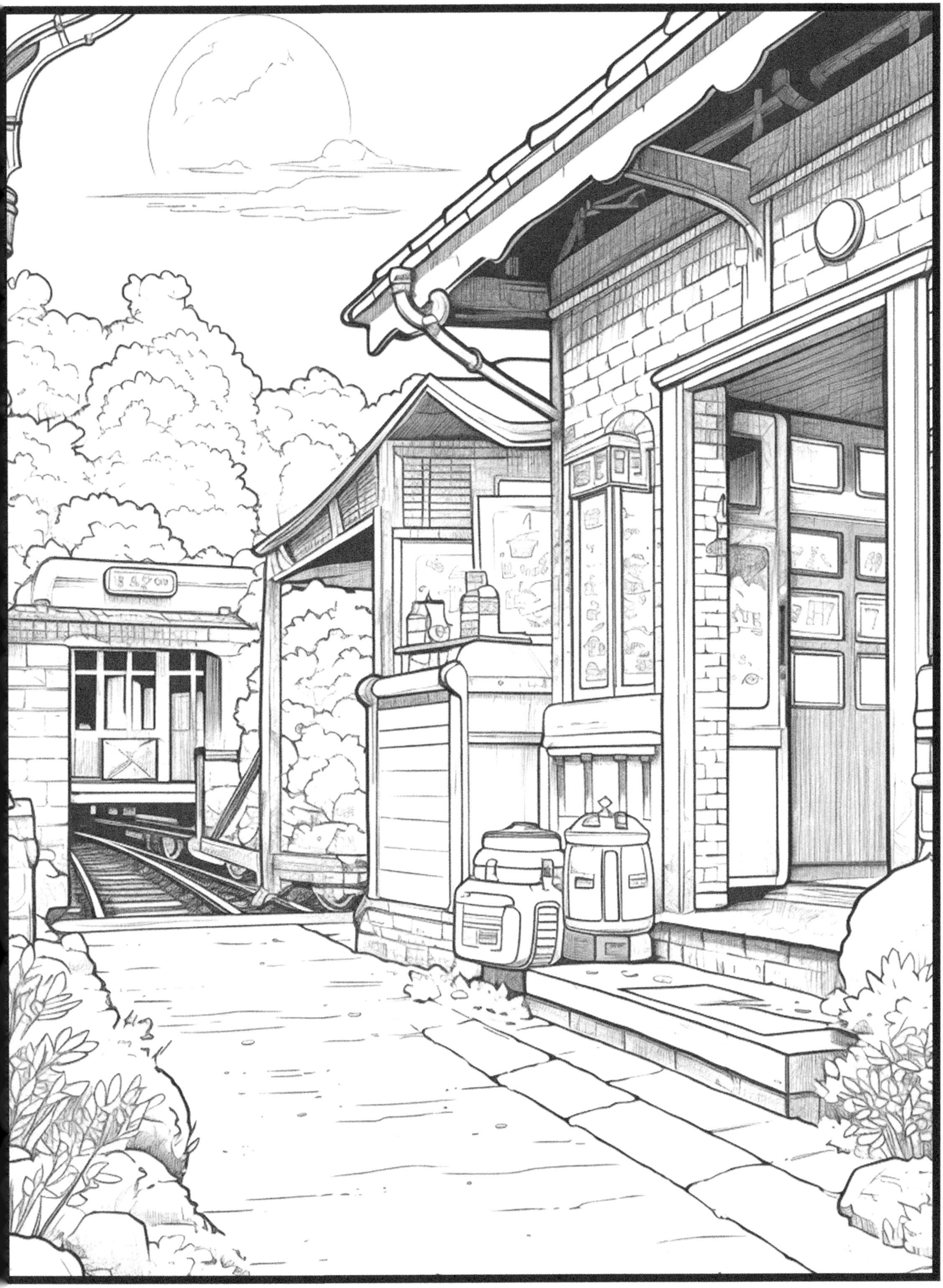

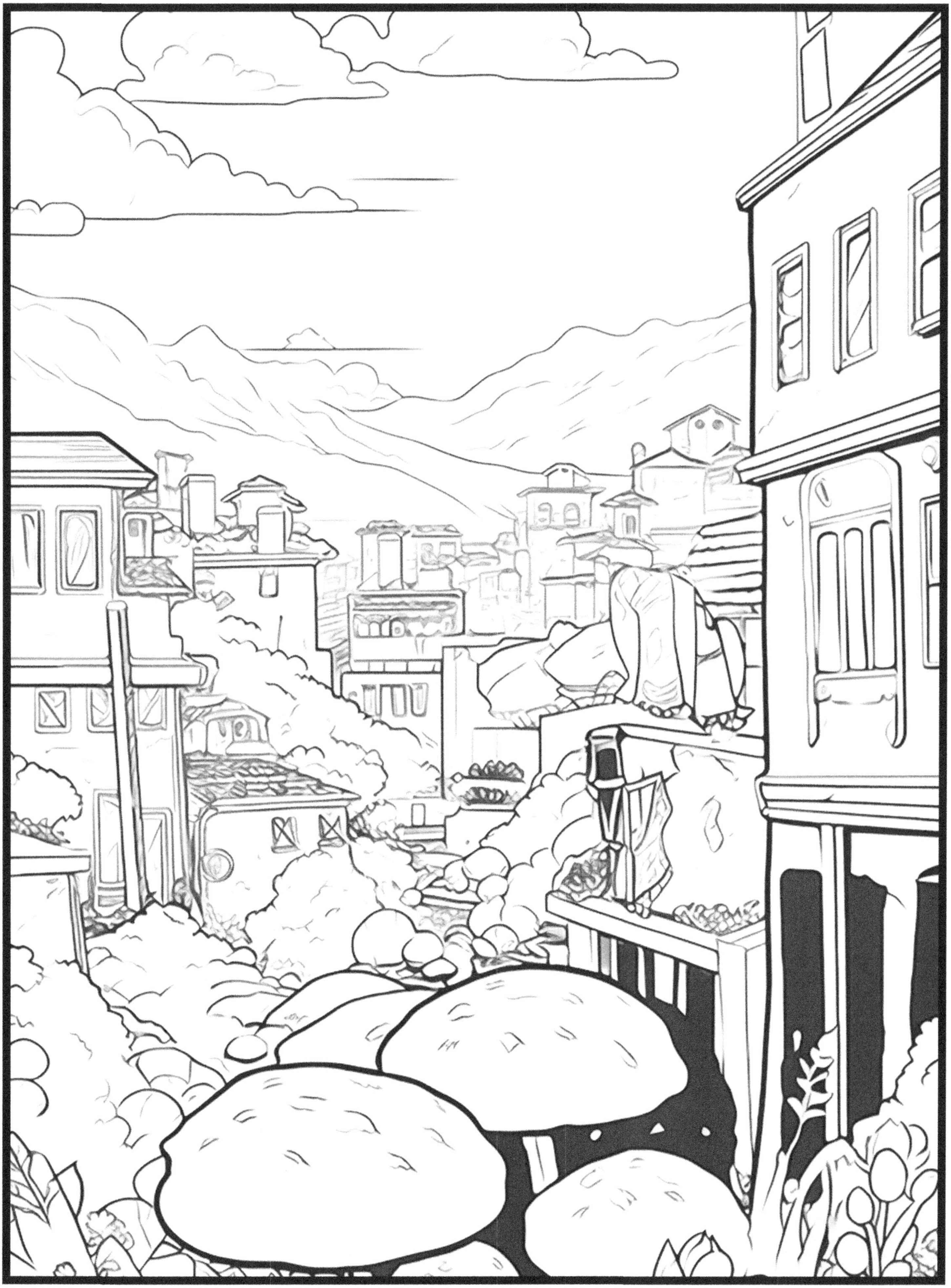

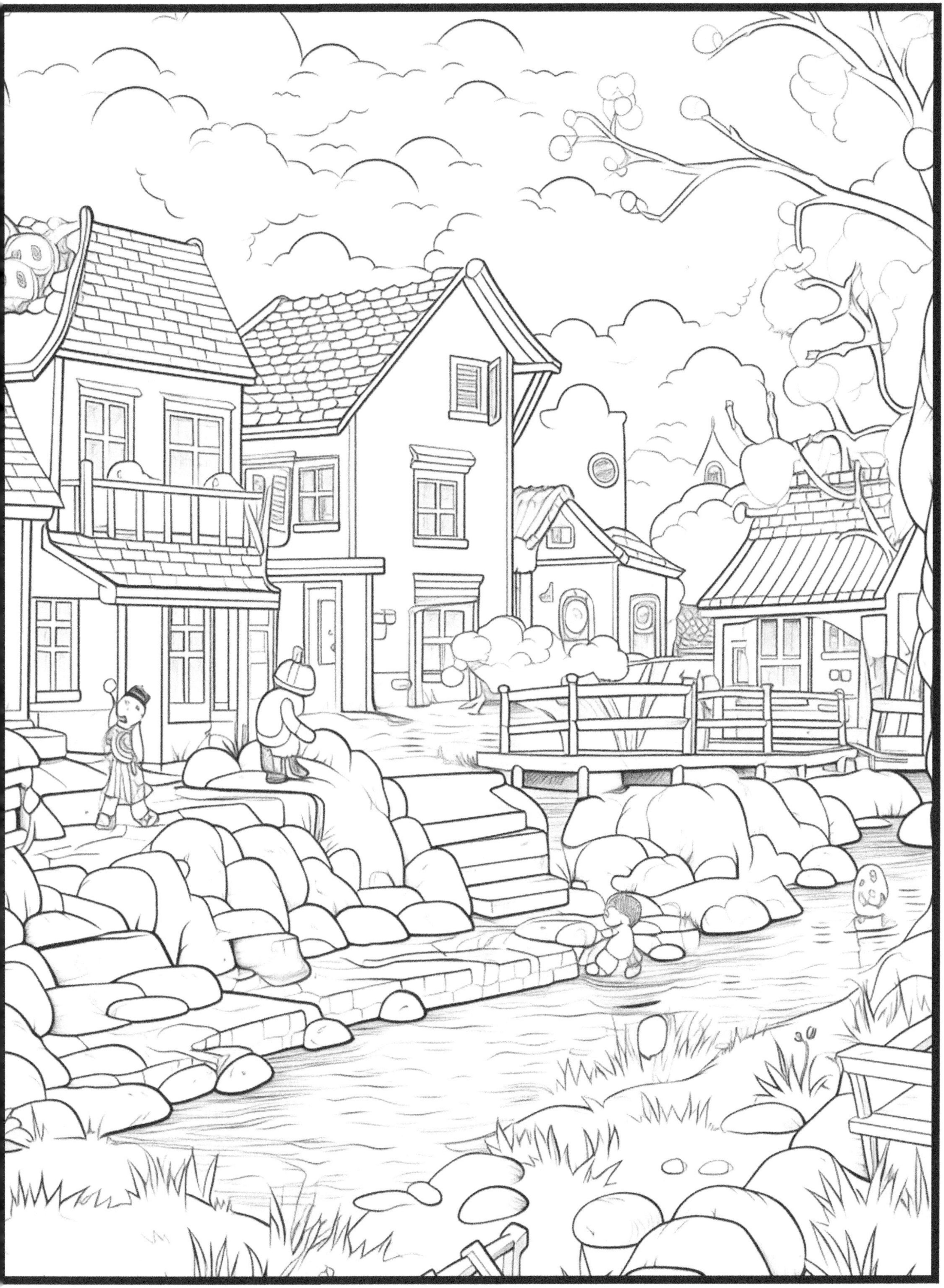

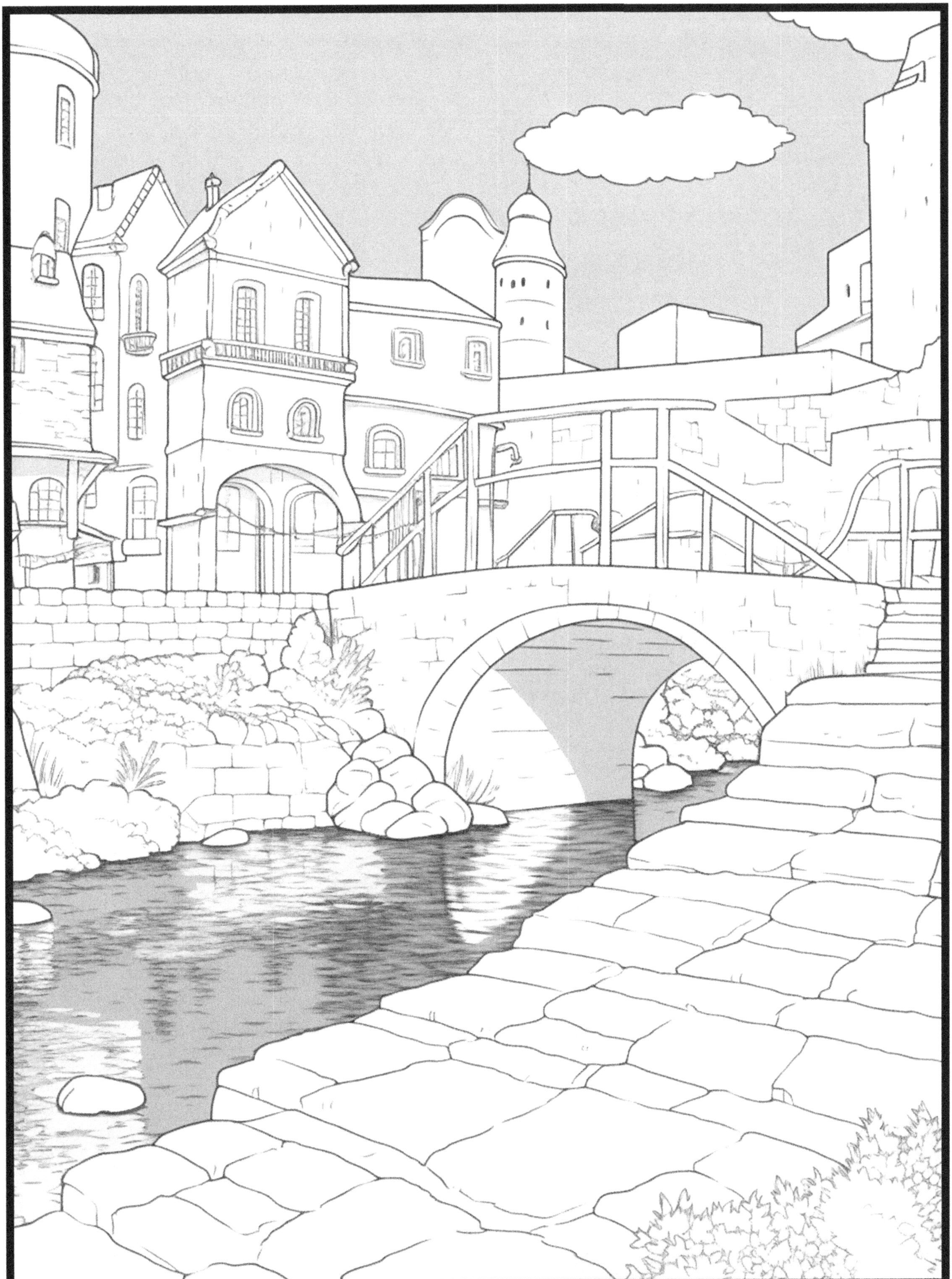

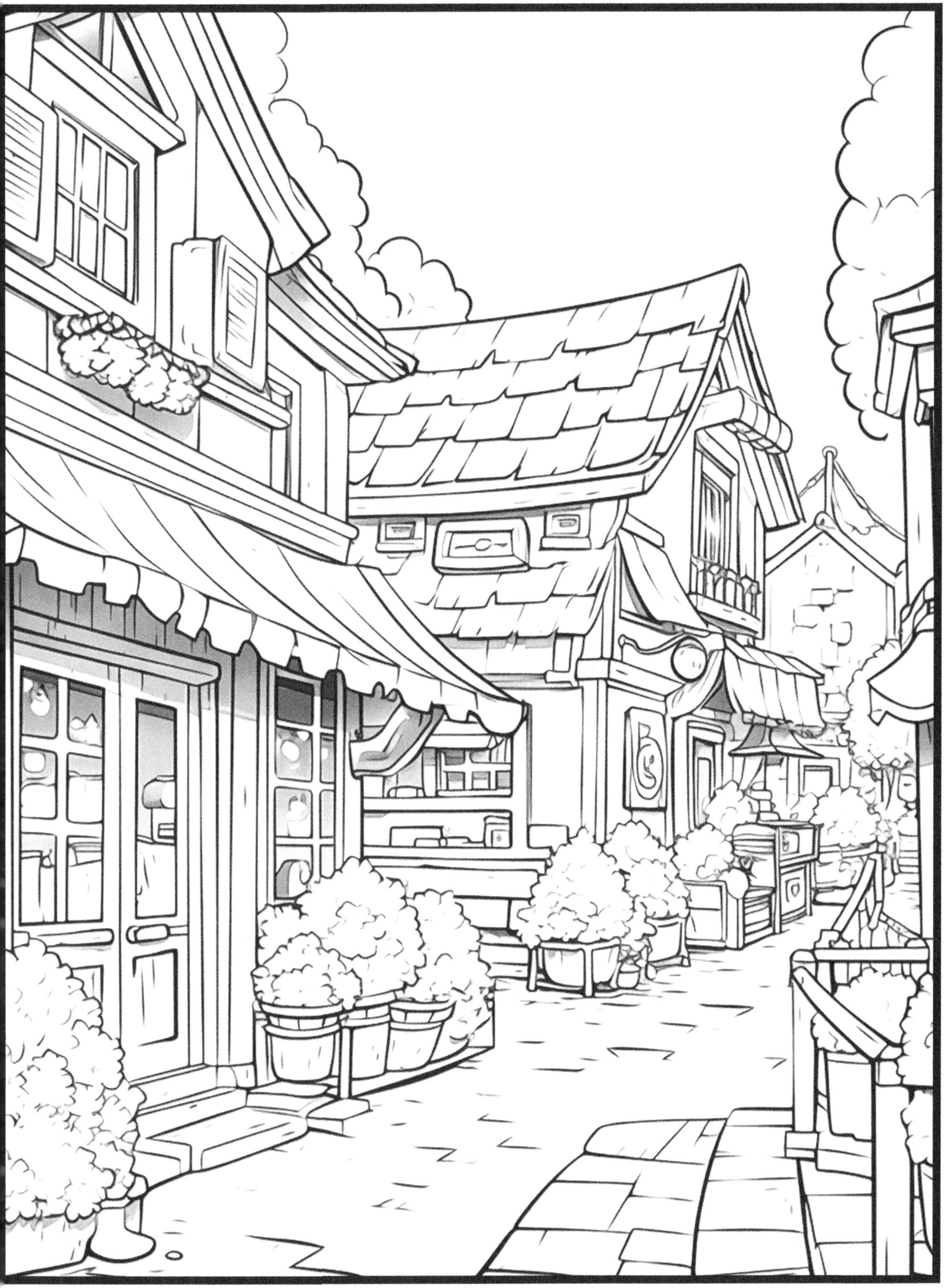

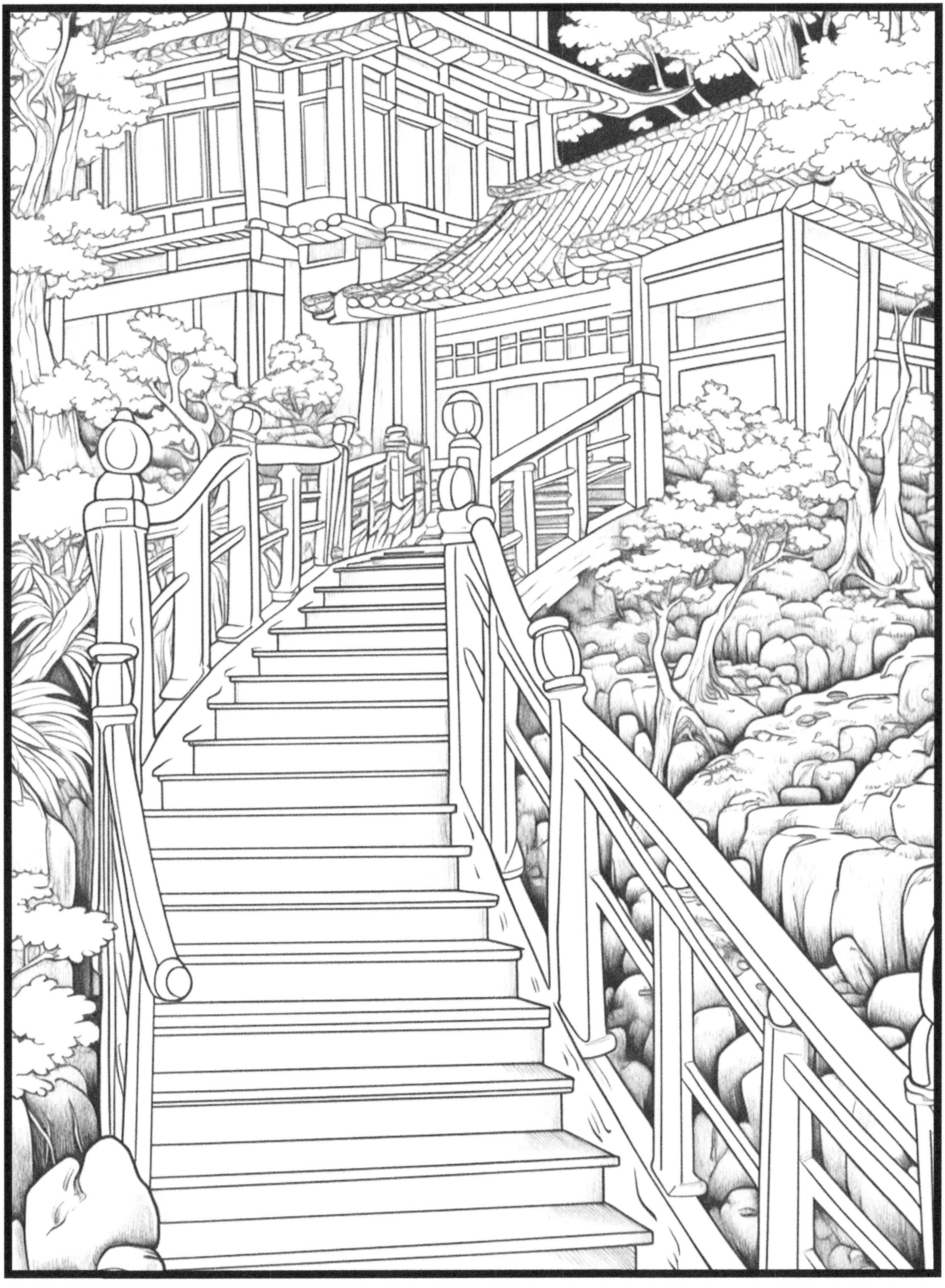

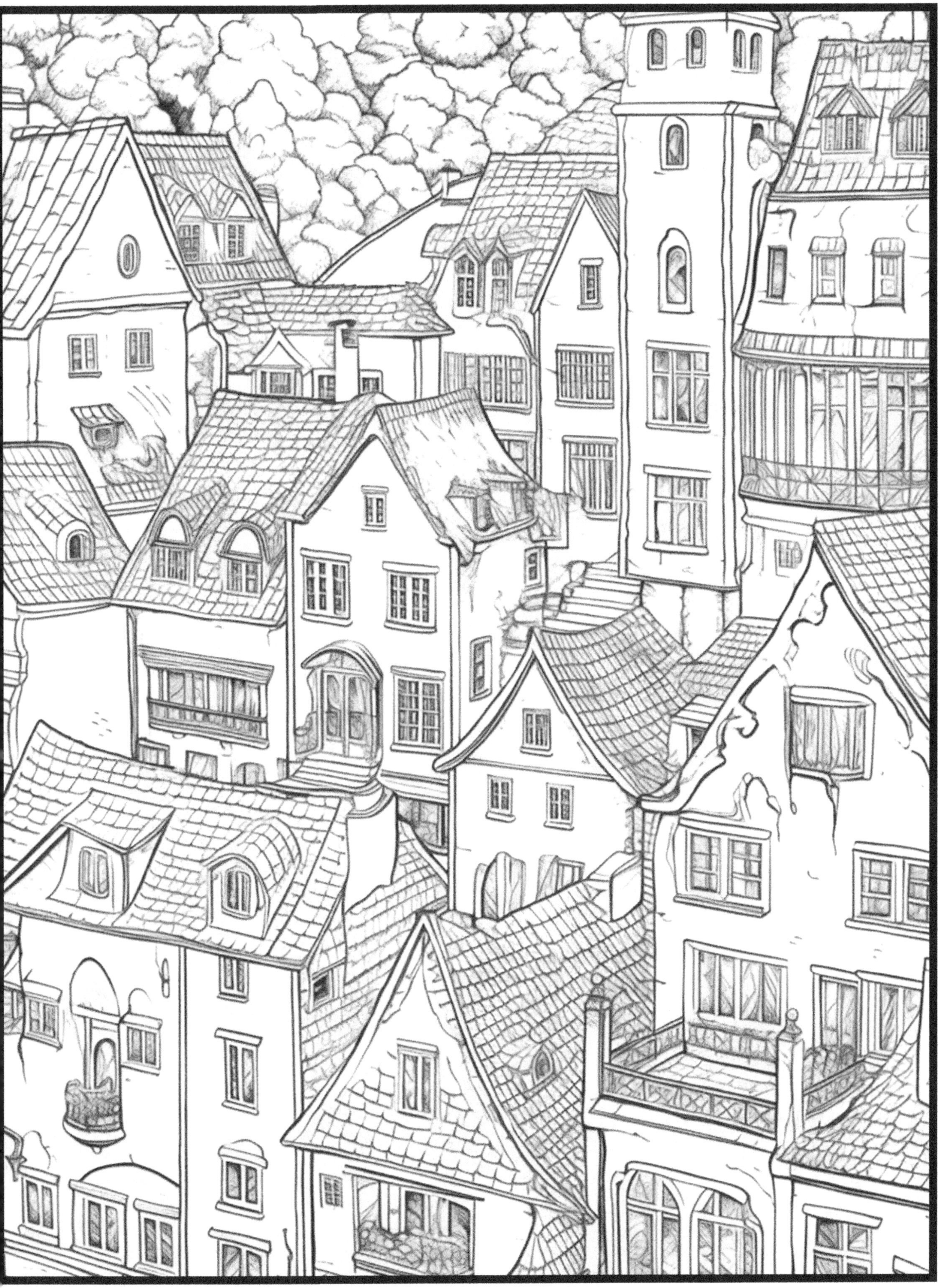

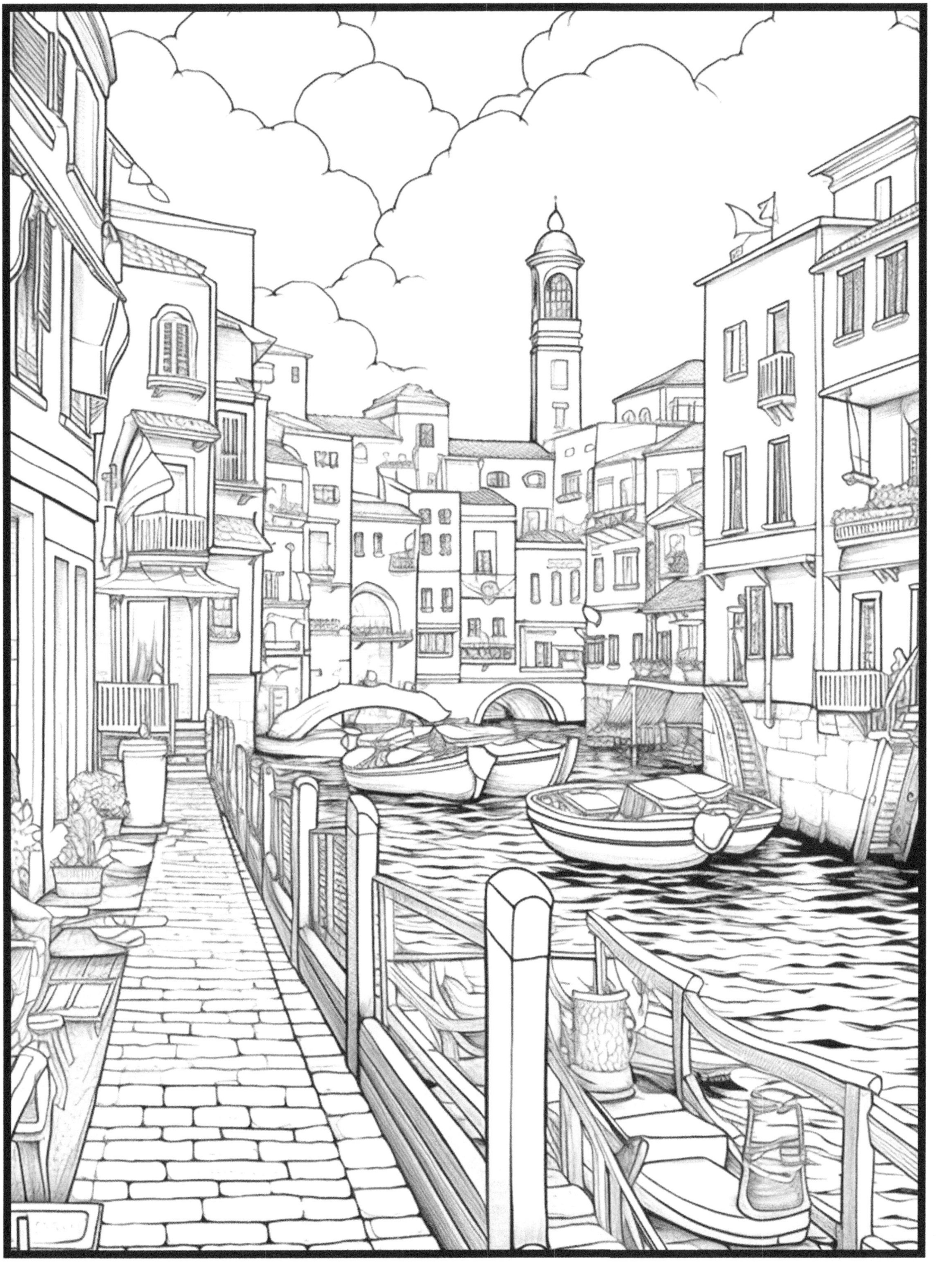

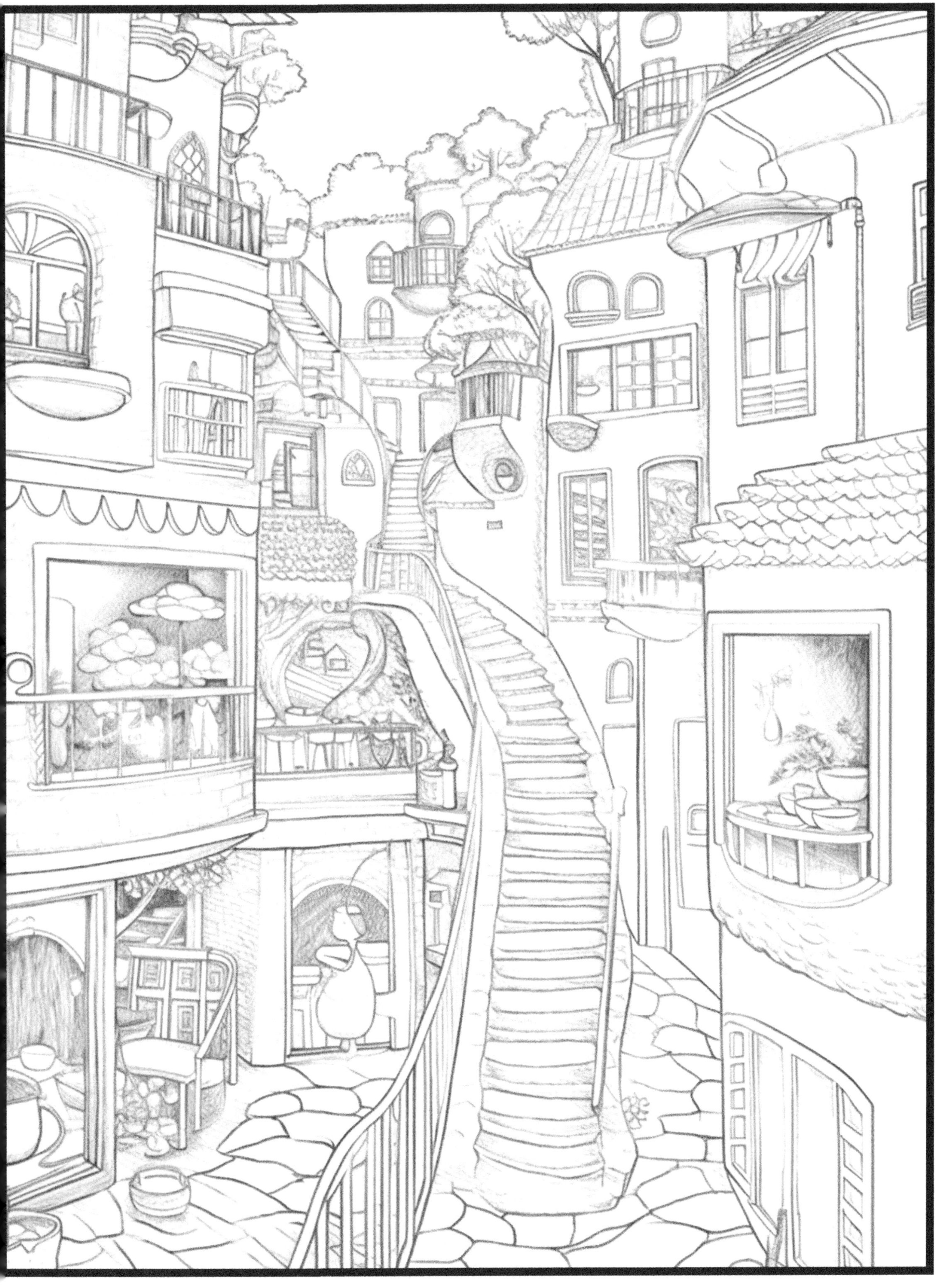

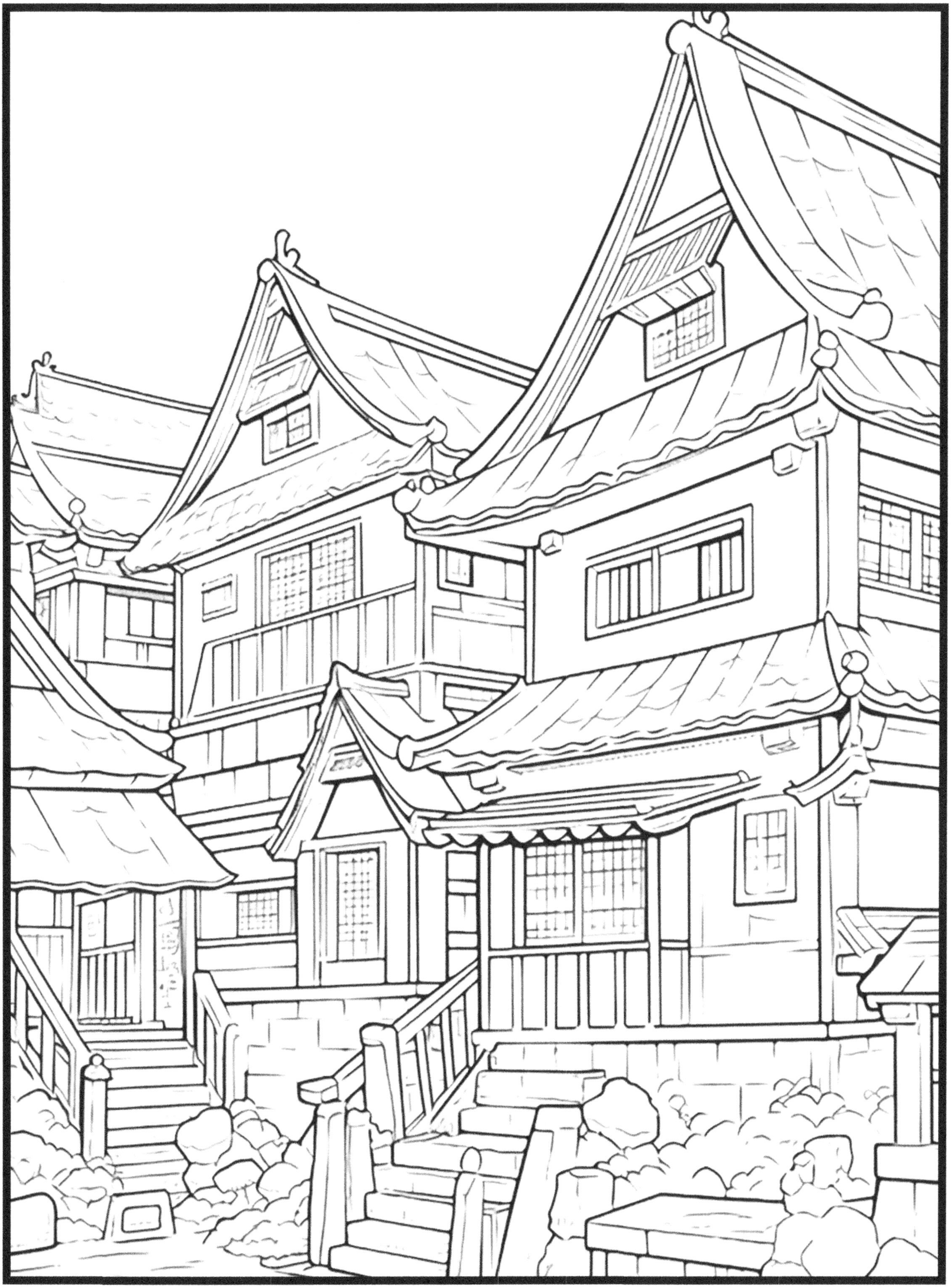

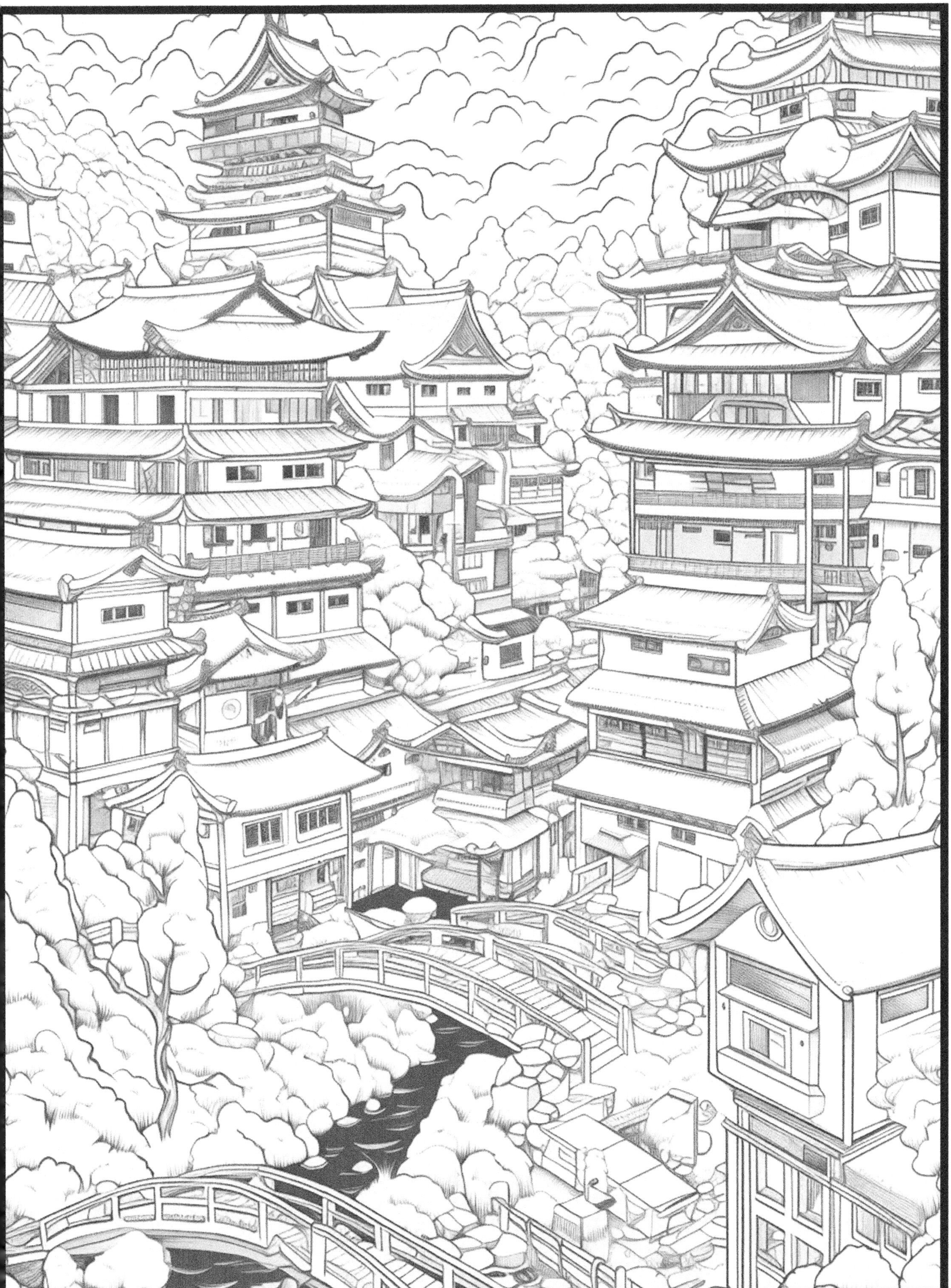

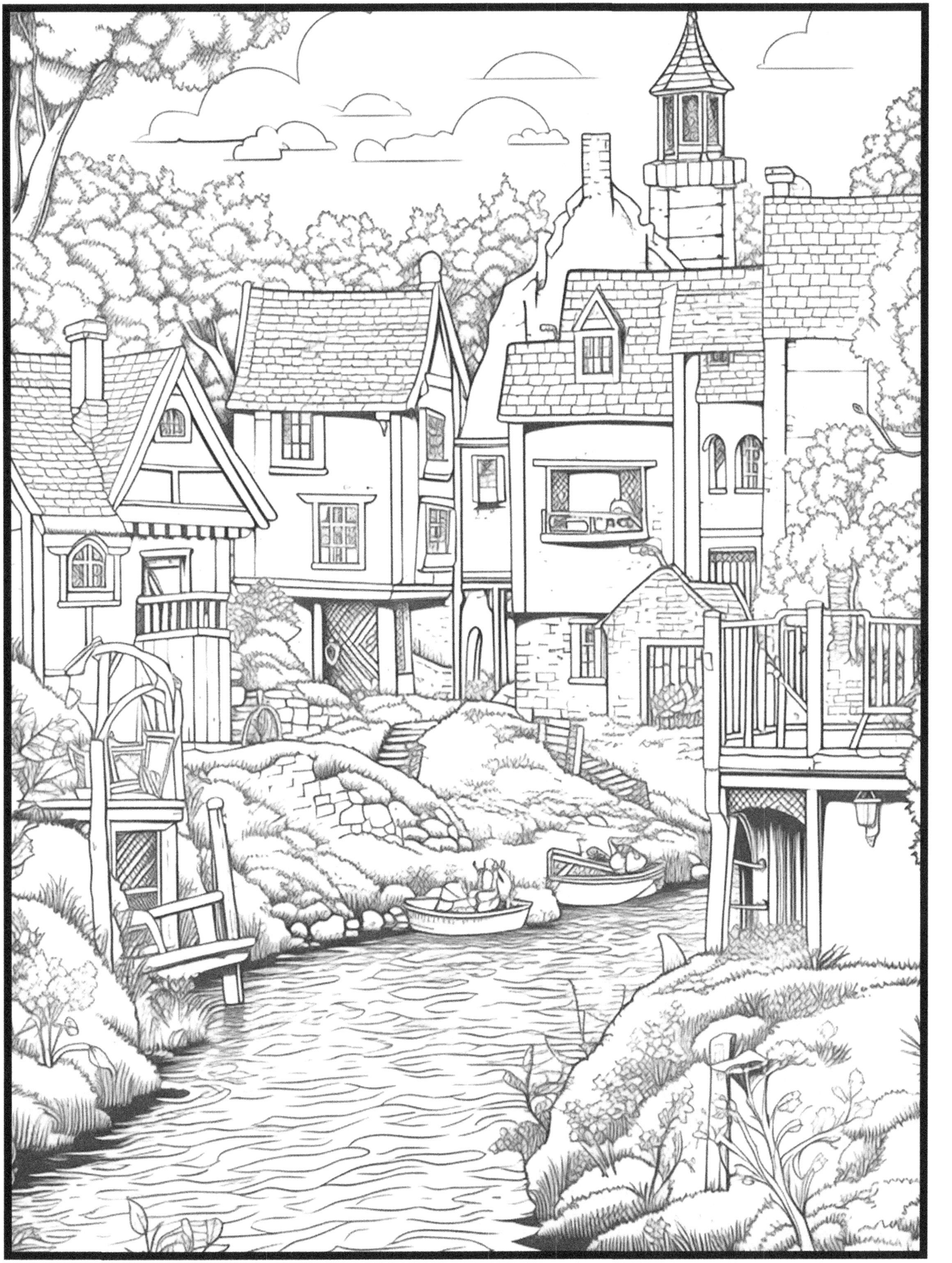

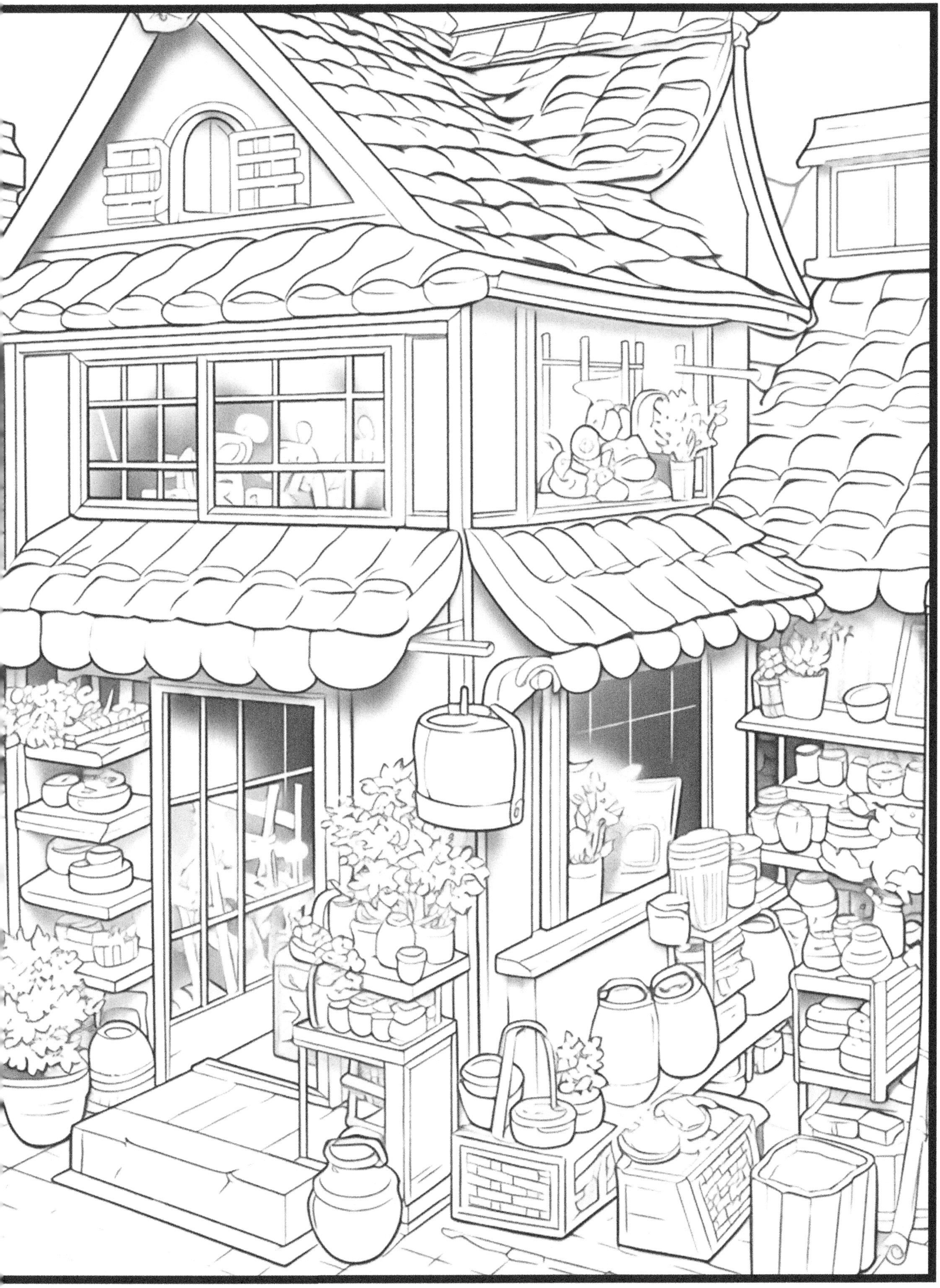

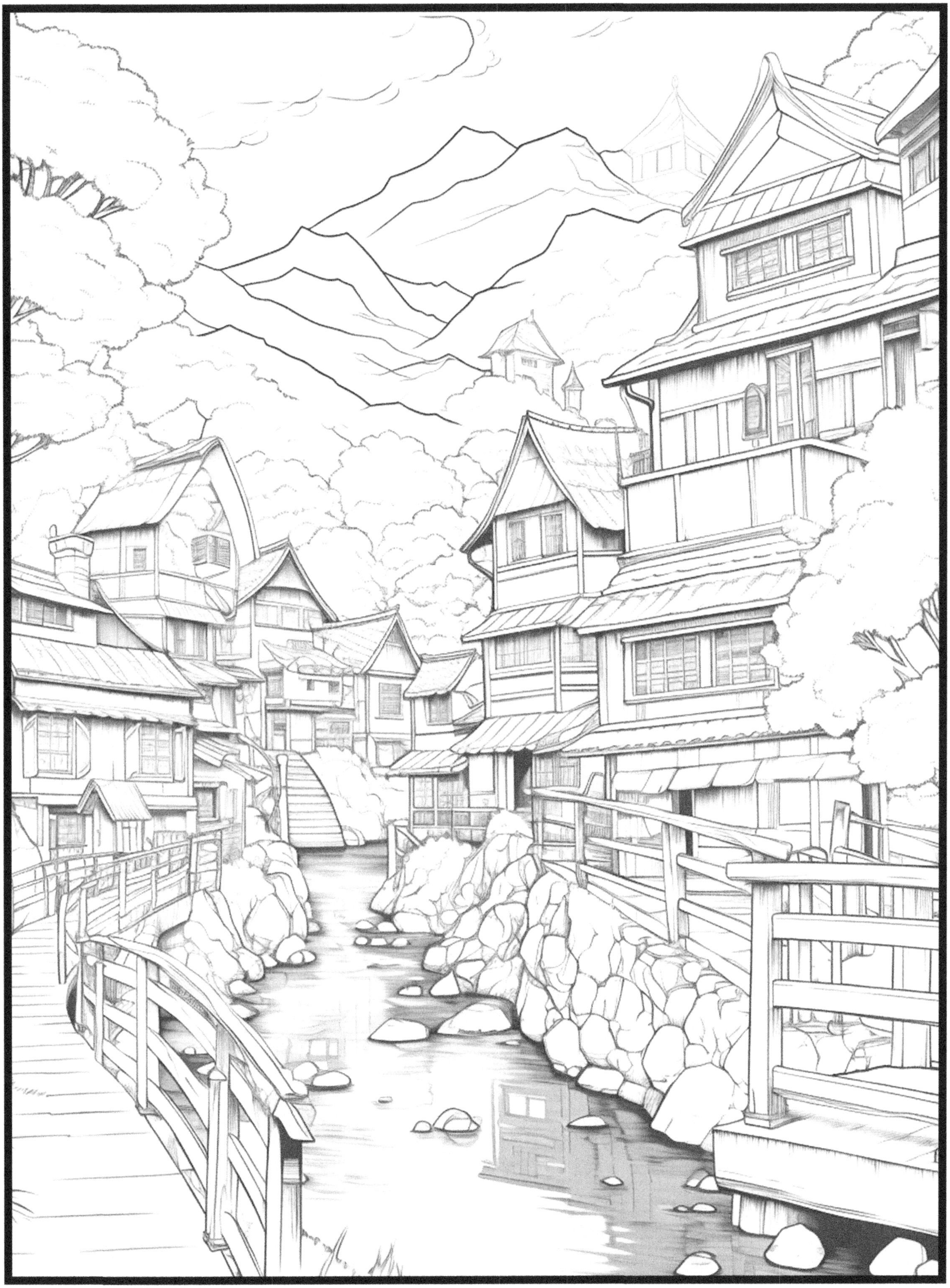

Made in the USA
Las Vegas, NV
19 January 2024

84605412R00037